COPY 23

89

J
BIOG
ZAPATA

Ragan, John David.
    Emiliano Zapata / John David Ragan. -- New
York : Chelsea House Publishers, c1989.

    111 p. : ill. ; bkl 6-9. -- (World leaders
past & present)   93804
    SUMMARY: A biography of the Mexican Indian
revolutionist whose main goal was to gain
land for his people.
    ISBN 1-555-46823-3(lib.bdg.) : $16.95

    1. Zapata, Emiliano, 1879-1919. 2.
Revolutionists. 3. Mexico--History--
Revolution, 1910-1920.   I. Title. II.
Series.

                            DEC 8 9 23
88-27326 /AC

EMILIANO ZAPATA

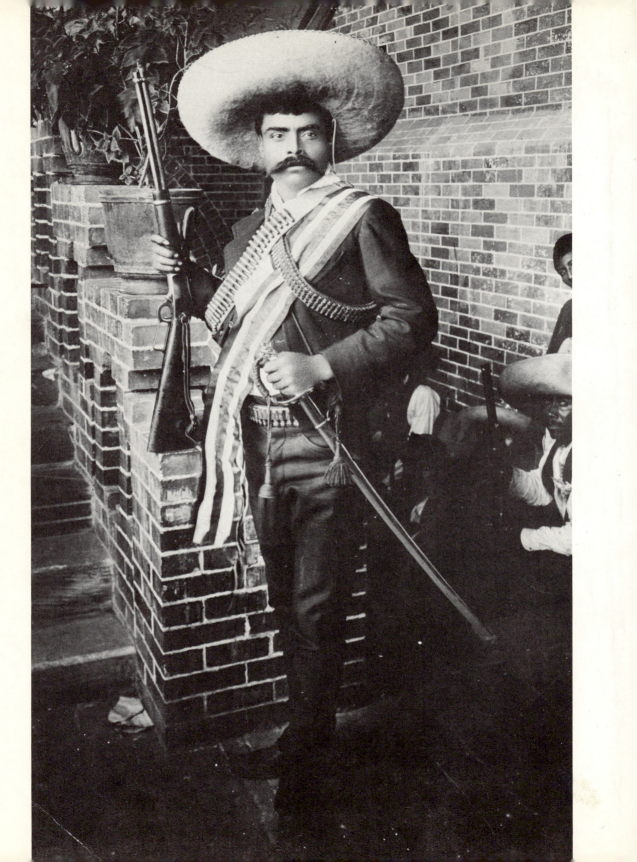

EMILIANO ZAPATA

John David Ragan

CHELSEA HOUSE PUBLISHERS

NEW YORK
PHILADELPHIA

Chelsea House Publishers
EDITOR-IN-CHIEF: Nancy Toff
EXECUTIVE EDITOR: Remmel T. Nunn
MANAGING EDITOR: Karyn Gullen Browne
COPY CHIEF: Juliann Barbato
PICTURE EDITOR: Adrian G. Allen
ART DIRECTOR: Maria Epes
MANUFACTURING MANAGER: Gerald Levine

World Leaders—Past & Present
SENIOR EDITOR: John W. Selfridge

Staff for EMILIANO ZAPATA
ASSOCIATE EDITOR: Jeff Klein
COPY EDITOR: Brian Sookram
DEPUTY COPY CHIEF: Ellen Scordato
EDITORIAL ASSISTANT: Heather Lewis
PICTURE RESEARCHER: Elie Porter
ASSISTANT ART DIRECTOR: Laurie Jewell
DESIGNER: David Murray
PRODUCTION COORDINATOR: Joseph Romano
COVER ILLUSTRATION: David Palladini

First Printing

1 3 5 7 9 8 6 4 2

Library of Congress Cataloging-in-Publication Data

Ragan, John David.
    Emiliano Zapata / John David Ragan.

    p.   cm.—(World leaders past & present)
    Bibliography: p.
    Includes index.
    Summary: A biography of the Mexican Indian revolutionist whose
main goal was to gain land for his people.
    ISBN 1-55546-823-3
        0-7910-0706-5 (pbk.)

    1. Zapata, Emiliano, 1879–1919—Juvenile literature.
2. Mexico—History—Revolution, 1910–1920—Juvenile
literature. 3. Revolutionists—Mexico—Biography—Juvenile
literature. 4. Generals—Mexico—Biography—Juvenile
literature. [1. Zapata, Emiliano, 1879–1919.
2. Revolutionists. 3. Mexico—History—Revolution,
1910–1920.] I. Title. II. Series.
F1234.Z37R34   1989   88-27326
972.08′1′0924—dc19   CIP
[B]   AC

Contents

JOHN ADAMS
JOHN QUINCY ADAMS
KONRAD ADENAUER
ALEXANDER THE GREAT
SALVADOR ALLENDE
MARC ANTONY
CORAZON AQUINO
YASIR ARAFAT
KING ARTHUR
HAFEZ al-ASSAD
KEMAL ATATÜRK
ATTILA
CLEMENT ATTLEE
AUGUSTUS CAESAR
MENACHEM BEGIN
DAVID BEN-GURION
OTTO VON BISMARCK
LÉON BLUM
SIMON BOLÍVAR
CESARE BORGIA
WILLY BRANDT
LEONID BREZHNEV
JULIUS CAESAR
JOHN CALVIN
JIMMY CARTER
FIDEL CASTRO
CATHERINE THE GREAT
CHARLEMAGNE
CHIANG KAI-SHEK
WINSTON CHURCHILL
GEORGES CLEMENCEAU
CLEOPATRA
CONSTANTINE THE GREAT
HERNÁN CORTÉS
OLIVER CROMWELL
GEORGES-JACQUES
    DANTON
JEFFERSON DAVIS
MOSHE DAYAN
CHARLES DE GAULLE
EAMON DE VALERA
EUGENE DEBS
DENG XIAOPING
BENJAMIN DISRAELI
ALEXANDER DUBČEK
FRANÇOIS & JEAN-CLAUDE
    DUVALIER
DWIGHT EISENHOWER
ELEANOR OF AQUITAINE
ELIZABETH I
FAISAL
FERDINAND & ISABELLA
FRANCISCO FRANCO
BENJAMIN FRANKLIN

FREDERICK THE GREAT
INDIRA GANDHI
MOHANDAS GANDHI
GIUSEPPE GARIBALDI
AMIN & BASHIR GEMAYEL
GENGHIS KHAN
WILLIAM GLADSTONE
MIKHAIL GORBACHEV
ULYSSES S. GRANT
ERNESTO "CHE" GUEVARA
TENZIN GYATSO
ALEXANDER HAMILTON
DAG HAMMARSKJÖLD
HENRY VIII
HENRY OF NAVARRE
PAUL VON HINDENBURG
HIROHITO
ADOLF HITLER
HO CHI MINH
KING HUSSEIN
IVAN THE TERRIBLE
ANDREW JACKSON
JAMES I
WOJCIECH JARUZELSKI
THOMAS JEFFERSON
JOAN OF ARC
POPE JOHN XXIII
POPE JOHN PAUL II
LYNDON JOHNSON
BENITO JUÁREZ
JOHN KENNEDY
ROBERT KENNEDY
JOMO KENYATTA
AYATOLLAH KHOMEINI
NIKITA KHRUSHCHEV
KIM IL SUNG
MARTIN LUTHER KING, JR.
HENRY KISSINGER
KUBLAI KHAN
LAFAYETTE
ROBERT E. LEE
VLADIMIR LENIN
ABRAHAM LINCOLN
DAVID LLOYD GEORGE
LOUIS XIV
MARTIN LUTHER
JUDAS MACCABEUS
JAMES MADISON
NELSON & WINNIE
    MANDELA
MAO ZEDONG
FERDINAND MARCOS
GEORGE MARSHALL

MARY, QUEEN OF SCOTS
TOMÁŠ MASARYK
GOLDA MEIR
KLEMENS VON METTERNICH
JAMES MONROE
HOSNI MUBARAK
ROBERT MUGABE
BENITO MUSSOLINI
NAPOLÉON BONAPARTE
GAMAL ABDEL NASSER
JAWAHARLAL NEHRU
NERO
NICHOLAS II
RICHARD NIXON
KWAME NKRUMAH
DANIEL ORTEGA
MOHAMMED REZA PAHLAVI
THOMAS PAINE
CHARLES STEWART
    PARNELL
PERICLES
JUAN PERÓN
PETER THE GREAT
POL POT
MUAMMAR EL-QADDAFI
RONALD REAGAN
CARDINAL RICHELIEU
MAXIMILIEN ROBESPIERRE
ELEANOR ROOSEVELT
FRANKLIN ROOSEVELT
THEODORE ROOSEVELT
ANWAR SADAT
HAILE SELASSIE
PRINCE SIHANOUK
JAN SMUTS
JOSEPH STALIN
SUKARNO
SUN YAT-SEN
TAMERLANE
MOTHER TERESA
MARGARET THATCHER
JOSIP BROZ TITO
TOUSSAINT L'OUVERTURE
LEON TROTSKY
PIERRE TRUDEAU
HARRY TRUMAN
QUEEN VICTORIA
LECH WALESA
GEORGE WASHINGTON
CHAIM WEIZMANN
WOODROW WILSON
XERXES
EMILIANO ZAPATA
ZHOU ENLAI

CHELSEA HOUSE PUBLISHERS

ON LEADERSHIP

Arthur M. Schlesinger, jr.

LEADERSHIP, it may be said, is really what makes the world go round. Love no doubt smooths the passage; but love is a private transaction between consenting adults. Leadership is a public transaction with history. The idea of leadership affirms the capacity of individuals to move, inspire, and mobilize masses of people so that they act together in pursuit of an end. Sometimes leadership serves good purposes, sometimes bad; but whether the end is benign or evil, great leaders are those men and women who leave their personal stamp on history.

Now, the very concept of leadership implies the proposition that individuals can make a difference. This proposition has never been universally accepted. From classical times to the present day, eminent thinkers have regarded individuals as no more than the agents and pawns of larger forces, whether the gods and goddesses of the ancient world or, in the modern era, race, class, nation, the dialectic, the will of the people, the spirit of the times, history itself. Against such forces, the individual dwindles into insignificance.

So contends the thesis of historical determinism. Tolstoy's great novel *War and Peace* offers a famous statement of the case. Why, Tolstoy asked, did millions of men in the Napoleonic Wars, denying their human feelings and their common sense, move back and forth across Europe slaughtering their fellows? "The war," Tolstoy answered, "was bound to happen simply because it was bound to happen." All prior history predetermined it. As for leaders, they, Tolstoy said, "are but the labels that serve to give a name to an end and, like labels, they have the least possible connection with the event." The greater the leader, "the more conspicuous the inevitability and the predestination of every act he commits." The leader, said Tolstoy, is "the slave of history."

Determinism takes many forms. Marxism is the determinism of class. Nazism the determinism of race. But the idea of men and women as the slaves of history runs athwart the deepest human instincts. Rigid determinism abolishes the idea of human freedom—

7

the assumption of free choice that underlies every move we make, every word we speak, every thought we think. It abolishes the idea of human responsibility, since it is manifestly unfair to reward or punish people for actions that are by definition beyond their control. No one can live consistently by any deterministic creed. The Marxist states prove this themselves by their extreme susceptibility to the cult of leadership.

More than that, history refutes the idea that individuals make no difference. In December 1931 a British politician crossing Park Avenue in New York City between 76th and 77th Streets around 10:30 P.M. looked in the wrong direction and was knocked down by an automobile—a moment, he later recalled, of a man aghast, a world aglare: "I do not understand why I was not broken like an eggshell or squashed like a gooseberry." Fourteen months later an American politician, sitting in an open car in Miami, Florida, was fired on by an assassin; the man beside him was hit. Those who believe that individuals make no difference to history might well ponder whether the next two decades would have been the same had Mario Constasino's car killed Winston Churchill in 1931 and Giuseppe Zangara's bullet killed Franklin Roosevelt in 1933. Suppose, in addition, that Adolf Hitler had been killed in the street fighting during the Munich *Putsch* of 1923 and that Lenin had died of typhus during World War I. What would the 20th century be like now?

For better or for worse, individuals do make a difference. "The notion that a people can run itself and its affairs anonymously," wrote the philosopher William James, "is now well known to be the silliest of absurdities. Mankind does nothing save through initiatives on the part of inventors, great or small, and imitation by the rest of us—these are the sole factors in human progress. Individuals of genius show the way, and set the patterns, which common people then adopt and follow."

Leadership, James suggests, means leadership in thought as well as in action. In the long run, leaders in thought may well make the greater difference to the world. But, as Woodrow Wilson once said, "Those only are leaders of men, in the general eye, who lead in action. . . . It is at their hands that new thought gets its translation into the crude language of deeds." Leaders in thought often invent in solitude and obscurity, leaving to later generations the tasks of imitation. Leaders in action—the leaders portrayed in this series—have to be effective in their own time.

And they cannot be effective by themselves. They must act in response to the rhythms of their age. Their genius must be adapted, in a phrase of William James's, "to the receptivities of the moment." Leaders are useless without followers. "There goes the mob," said the French politician hearing a clamor in the streets. "I am their leader. I must follow them." Great leaders turn the inchoate emotions of the mob to purposes of their own. They seize on the opportunities of their time, the hopes, fears, frustrations, crises, potentialities. They succeed when events have prepared the way for them, when the community is awaiting to be aroused, when they can provide the clarifying and organizing ideas. Leadership ignites the circuit between the individual and the mass and thereby alters history.

It may alter history for better or for worse. Leaders have been responsible for the most extravagant follies and most monstrous crimes that have beset suffering humanity. They have also been vital in such gains as humanity has made in individual freedom, religious and racial tolerance, social justice, and respect for human rights.

There is no sure way to tell in advance who is going to lead for good and who for evil. But a glance at the gallery of men and women in *World Leaders—Past and Present* suggests some useful tests.

One test is this: Do leaders lead by force or by persuasion? By command or by consent? Through most of history leadership was exercised by the divine right of authority. The duty of followers was to defer and to obey. "Theirs not to reason why / Theirs but to do and die." On occasion, as with the so-called enlightened despots of the 18th century in Europe, absolutist leadership was animated by humane purposes. More often, absolutism nourished the passion for domination, land, gold, and conquest and resulted in tyranny.

The great revolution of modern times has been the revolution of equality. The idea that all people should be equal in their legal condition has undermined the old structure of authority, hierarchy, and deference. The revolution of equality has had two contrary effects on the nature of leadership. For equality, as Alexis de Tocqueville pointed out in his great study *Democracy in America*, might mean equality in servitude as well as equality in freedom.

"I know of only two methods of establishing equality in the political world," Tocqueville wrote. "Rights must be given to every citizen, or none at all to anyone . . . save one, who is the master of all." There was no middle ground "between the sovereignty of all and the absolute power of one man." In his astonishing prediction of 20th-century totalitarian dictatorship, Tocqueville explained how the revolution of equality could lead to the *"Führerprinzip"* and more terrible absolutism than the world had ever known.

But when rights are given to every citizen and the sovereignty of all is established, the problem of leadership takes a new form, becomes more exacting than ever before. It is easy to issue commands and enforce them by the rope and the stake, the concentration camp and the *gulag.* It is much harder to use argument and achievement to overcome opposition and win consent. The Founding Fathers of the United States understood the difficulty. They believed that history had given them the opportunity to decide, as Alexander Hamilton wrote in the first Federalist Paper, whether men are indeed capable of basing government on "reflection and choice, or whether they are forever destined to depend . . . on accident and force."

Government by reflection and choice called for a new style of leadership and a new quality of followership. It required leaders to be responsive to popular concerns, and it required followers to be active and informed participants in the process. Democracy does not eliminate emotion from politics; sometimes it fosters demagoguery; but it is confident that, as the greatest of democratic leaders put it, you cannot fool all of the people all of the time. It measures leadership by results and retires those who overreach or falter or fail.

It is true that in the long run despots are measured by results too. But they can postpone the day of judgment, sometimes indefinitely, and in the meantime they can do infinite harm. It is also true that democracy is no guarantee of virtue and intelligence in government, for the voice of the people is not necessarily the voice of God. But democracy, by assuring the right of opposition, offers built-in resistance to the evils inherent in absolutism. As the theologian Reinhold Niebuhr summed it up, "Man's capacity for justice makes democracy possible, but man's inclination to injustice makes democracy necessary."

A second test for leadership is the end for which power is sought. When leaders have as their goal the supremacy of a master race or the promotion of totalitarian revolution or the acquisition and exploitation of colonies or the protection of greed and privilege or the preservation of personal power, it is likely that their leadership will do little to advance the cause of humanity. When their goal is the abolition of slavery, the liberation of women, the enlargement of opportunity for the poor and powerless, the extension of equal rights to racial minorities, the defense of the freedoms of expression and opposition, it is likely that their leadership will increase the sum of human liberty and welfare.

10

Leaders have done great harm to the world. They have also conferred great benefits. You will find both sorts in this series. Even "good" leaders must be regarded with a certain wariness. Leaders are not demigods; they put on their trousers one leg after another just like ordinary mortals. No leader is infallible, and every leader needs to be reminded of this at regular intervals. Irreverence irritates leaders but is their salvation. Unquestioning submission corrupts leaders and demeans followers. Making a cult of a leader is always a mistake. Fortunately hero worship generates its own antidote. "Every hero," said Emerson, "becomes a bore at last."

The signal benefit the great leaders confer is to embolden the rest of us to live according to our own best selves, to be active, insistent, and resolute in affirming our own sense of things. For great leaders attest to the reality of human freedom against the supposed inevitabilities of history. And they attest to the wisdom and power that may lie within the most unlikely of us, which is why Abraham Lincoln remains the supreme example of great leadership. A great leader, said Emerson, exhibits new possibilities to all humanity. "We feed on genius. . . . Great men exist that there may be greater men."

Great leaders, in short, justify themselves by emancipating and empowering their followers. So humanity struggles to master its destiny, remembering with Alexis de Tocqueville: "It is true that around every man a fatal circle is traced beyond which he cannot pass; but within the wide verge of that circle he is powerful and free; as it is with man, so with communities."

1

A Revolution Begins

On the evening of March 11, 1911, a group of armed men broke into the police station of Villa de Ayala, a small village in southern Mexico. They quickly disarmed the police and held a meeting in the town square, where they enlisted about 70 men into their revolt. By the next morning they were pounding down the Cuautla River valley on horseback, their ranks steadily growing as they passed through villages and ranchos where hundreds of local people joined them. It was a loosely organized group, led by a number of men. One of them was named Emiliano Zapata.

Only 31 years old, Zapata was already a trusted leader, president of the village council of Anenecuilco, and one of the finest horsemen in the state of Morelos. His penetrating eyes and intense, watchful face gave him an air of stubborn persistence. In the past he had been in frequent conflict with the authorities over the confiscation of lands belonging

Poor Mexico. So far from God and so near the United States.
—PORFIRIO DÍAZ
Mexican president

Emiliano Zapata, leader of the peasant revolution in the Mexican state of Morelos from 1910 to 1919. Zapata successfully fought for land reform and the traditional rights of small farmers and villagers.

General Porfirio Díaz, dictator of Mexico from 1877 to 1880 and from 1884 to 1910. Díaz encouraged U.S. and European investment in Mexican land and industry, balancing the national budget and bringing prosperity to the nation's upper classes, but at the expense of the peasants who made up the majority of the population.

to his village. Now Zapata, his fellow leaders, and this rapidly forming army of small farmers and sharecroppers had openly declared themselves against the government. Their revolt would make the question of land for small peasant farmers one of the most important issues of the Mexican Revolution.

Zapata and the villagers of Morelos were not the only ones plotting revolt. Throughout Mexico, to the cry of "¡Qué viva la revolución!" ("Long live the revolution!"), men were banding together to attack government troops. The rebel leaders Francisco "Pancho" Villa and Pascual Orozco had been fighting the government in northern Mexico since November 1910, and in February 1911, Francisco Madero, the chief of the revolutionary movement, had returned to Mexico from political exile in the United States. Everywhere in the country, young men like Lázaro Cárdenas, 15 years old and a future president of Mexico, broke into local jails, released prisoners, seized guns, and headed for the hills to join the movement.

The common enemy of these revolutionaries was Porfirio Díaz, the dictator who had ruled Mexico for 34 years. He had first seized power in a military coup in 1876 and since then had been regularly reelected the nation's president in methodically rigged elections. With his powerful political machine and his *rurales* (state police), Díaz had brought stability to Mexico after 75 years of war and revolution.

To stimulate the nation's economy, Díaz had given extensive tax-free concessions to foreign investors, attracting more than $1.5 billion of U.S. investment to Mexico. American interests owned 90 percent of Mexico's mining industry, as well as large plantations producing export crops such as sugar, cotton, and tobacco. Foreign businessmen had financed the construction of an extensive railway system, which in turn had spurred the rapid proliferation of textile mills, mining operations, and large-scale commercial agriculture. By 1910, the federal budget was balanced, the treasury had a huge surplus, and Mexico's foreign trade was 10 times greater than it had been before Díaz.

Francisco Madero, the leader of the Mexican revolutionary movement. A moderate seeking an end to Díaz's rule and the reinstitution of democracy, Madero tried to balance the interests of the peasant farmers of the south with the cattle herders of the north and the liberal middle class.

The northern rebel leaders Pancho Villa (left, in white hat) and Pascual Orozco (right, in sombrero). Villa, a herder and bandit leader, and Orozco, who was killed by Texas Rangers in 1912, headed revolutionary armies that battled government forces in the north while Zapata fought federal troops in the south.

Díaz's economic strategy had been devised by foreign consultants and by a small group of wealthy Mexican advisers who were called *científicos*, because they were managing the country in a modern, "scientific" way. The científicos, as well as the Mexican upper classes and the foreign investors, had prospered under Díaz and provided him with his strongest support.

Yet there was a problem: The nation's financial progress had been achieved at a terrible cost to the majority of the Mexican people. The benefits of the system went primarily to the foreign investors and to the small proportion of Mexicans involved in the Díaz regime. But for the villagers and small farmers of Indian blood who made up the vast majority of the population, times could hardly have been worse.

With the encouragement of the Díaz regime, the large landed estates called *haciendas* had expanded rapidly as hacienda owners seized land from villagers and small farmers. The hacienda owners took common lands traditionally held by the villages for grazing and farming, as well as private plots owned by small farmers. The farmers were constantly called into court to prove ownership, but the courts were controlled by the hacienda owners and usually decided in their favor. Even when the court ruled against the hacienda owners they sometimes simply occupied the villagers' land by force.

By 1910, 96 percent of Mexico's rural families owned no land, and fewer than 1,000 powerful landowners controlled the agricultural resources of a country of more than 12 million people. Some of the rural estates exceeded 6 million acres in size, larger than the state of Massachusetts or the nation of El Salvador.

Once a Mexican peasant had lost his land, he had no choice but to go to work as a laborer on the large estates. There he was often forced to live on the hacienda, to buy his food and clothing at the hacienda store, and to accept whatever wages the owner offered. If he fell into debt to the estate owner, he was legally bound to the hacienda and required to work there until his debt was paid off, making him, in effect, a "debt slave." If the debt was not paid off in his lifetime, it was passed on to his children who were also legally bound to the land as debt slaves.

A single bad harvest could put a peasant in debt. And because the landowner set the prices at the hacienda store, set the wages, kept the accounts, and was responsible for deciding when the debt was paid off, he could easily keep the peasant and his children in debt forever.

By the end of the Díaz regime, 60 percent of the people in Mexico were debt slaves. On the great plantations of the Yucatán in the southeast, or in the tobacco-growing areas of Valle Nacional in the south, they were commonly bought and sold for about $45 a head. In these areas, the debt slaves were kept in great roofed pens made of wooden slats woven together with barbed wire. Their families were intentionally broken up and sold to different masters to break their resistance. Conditions in Valle Nacional were so bad that the average debt slave lasted only about seven months before he died and had to be replaced. The Mexican army depopulated whole areas of the country in their wars against the Maya and Yaqui Indians, capturing and selling the Indians as debt slaves at a lucrative profit. The police sold their prisoners in the same way.

> *Porfirio's government took everything away from us. Everything went to the rich, the hacendados, those with the power were the masters and we had nothing.*
> —PEDRO MARTINEZ
> a Mexican peasant and Zapata supporter

The Díaz regime had pushed most of rural Mexico to the point where its people had nothing to lose. Corruption and bribery were rampant, 75 percent of the people were illiterate, and the rural population was undergoing a rapid process of impoverishment. Mexico was a powder keg of poverty and injustice, waiting to explode.

The Zapatista revolution would be made not by the poorest Mexicans, but by small farmers like Zapata and the people from his village. They still had their freedom and some property, which gave them the means and the independence to resist. Furthermore, they saw that because of the way things were going they would soon lose everything.

Zapata was just one of a number of revolutionary leaders in the north and south of the country. The rebel commander in Morelos was a village school-

A scene on a hacienda, or large estate. In Morelos, hacienda owners expanded the size of their estates by appropriating land long held communally by villages or individually by small farmers. By 1910, 96 percent of Mexico's rural families were without land; most were forced to work for exceedingly low wages on haciendas.

master who was chosen because he could read, write, and speak well. On March 24, 1911, the peasant army moved toward its first objective, the town of Jojutla, the government forces fled to the state capital, Cuernavaca. The rebels entered the abandoned town and some of them began to burn and loot, defying the orders of the schoolmaster commander, who called on Zapata to help him to restore order. Order was restored with some difficulty, but the furious commander resigned his position and returned home with his two sons. On the way, they were arrested and shot by an enemy patrol.

It was under these circumstances that Zapata emerged as leader of the revolt. He was not a great speaker, and at meetings he listened silently while the others talked and argued; after everyone had finished, he would quietly express his opinion in a

> *We were completely enslaved by the hacendados. That is what Zapata fought to set right.*
> —PEDRO MARTINEZ
> a Mexican peasant and
> Zapata supporter

few words. There was an intensity and a carefulness about him that inspired trust and made him an accepted arbitrator. A villager of mixed Spanish and Indian blood, like many of his followers, Zapata commanded his men only by their consent, and was respected and obeyed. He now took command of the disorganized army and returned to the hills.

After more than a month of reorganization and contacts with other leaders supporting the revolution, the army moved out of the hills. They took the small town of Yautepec, using young "dynamite boys" who pretended to be playing as they moved toward the army guardhouse, then threw bombs through the windows. As the bombs exploded, the Zapatistas charged into the square on horseback, taking the building. On May 13, 1911, the Zapatistas attacked Cuautla — one of the largest towns in Morelos and located only a few miles from Zapata's village of Anenecuilco — and took it after five days of desperate, house-to-house fighting. The town was defended by a ring of machine-gun nests, which the Zapatistas charged, on horseback and on foot, using dynamite bombs and rifles as they fought their way toward the center of town. Zapata lost nearly a third of his men, who were killed or wounded in a battle that left the town a gutted wreck.

Refugees from rural states standing in a soup line at a Mexico City Red Cross station. Under policies encouraged by the Díaz government, peasants who lost their land and were forced to work on haciendas usually went into permanent debt to the hacienda owners. By 1910, 60 percent of all Mexicans were "debt slaves."

As soon as the battle of Cuautla had been won, Zapata wrote to the presidents of the local village councils and authorized them to begin reoccupying lands illegally seized by the haciendas. He promised the full support of the Zapatista army and immediately sent out detachments of troops to aid in the reoccupation. As the planting season started, peasants throughout the sections of Morelos controlled by the Zapatistas began breaking down hacienda walls and cultivating the lands that they had lost to the large estates.

On May 25, 1911, President Díaz, his regime disintegrating in the face of widespread revolt, gave up. He left Mexico City for the coast, where a German steamship was waiting to take him into exile. Five days later Zapata's army made a triumphant entry into Cuernavaca to join other rebel leaders who had already entered the city. In the flush of victory, it seemed that Zapata and his villagers had won. They did not know that their struggle for land reform was only beginning.

Men standing in the ruins of a house in the Morelos town of Yautepec in 1911. The Zapatista revolt began in March 1911, five months after the northern rebels had started fighting the central government. By the middle of the year the Zapatista uprising had escalated into full-scale warfare throughout Morelos.

Eufemio Zapata   Grab.

2

The Birth of a Dream

Emiliano Zapata was born in the southern Mexican village of Anenecuilco, probably in 1879 (the date is uncertain because the village's church records were destroyed during the revolution), to parents who were both of mixed Spanish and Indian blood. He appears to have been one of the youngest of 10 children, only 4 or 5 of whom survived to become adults.

The Zapatas' modest house was a solid building made of stone and adobe with a thatched roof and dirt floor; the central structure measured about 12 feet by 14 feet, with small adjoining rooms attached to it. The cooking was done in a large clay oven and the family's diet consisted largely of corn tortillas and beans. From time to time they also had milk, meat, eggs, cheese, and butter, which they produced themselves and often sold locally. The family made their living raising and breeding horses and cattle, which they pastured on the drier land to the west of the river running through the village.

Like a wound, the country's history opens in Anenecuilco.
—GASTÓN GARCÍA CANTÓ

Emiliano Zapata (right) and his brother Eufemio in 1913. Emiliano was born in the Morelos village of Anenecuilco in about 1879 to a modestly successful family of farmers and horse breeders. Like most Morelos villagers, the Zapatas were of mixed Spanish and Indian ancestry.

Conquistadores under the direction of a Catholic priest pull down a statue of an Aztec god during the Spanish conquest of Mexico in the early 1500s. Mexican Indians suffered greatly under Spanish rule, which lasted until 1821, but retained much of their culture and social structure in rural areas such as Morelos.

As successful stockbreeders the Zapatas were better off than most people in the village and did not have to work as laborers on the hacienda. They grew most of their food on small plots of land that they owned, and their children earned extra money by tending other people's cattle and taking them to pasture.

The Zapatas lived in a country with a long and turbulent history. For nearly 2,000 years Mexico had been ruled by a series of Indian empires, many of them highly developed civilizations, before being conquered by the Spanish in the 16th century. Mexico's Indian heritage had not disappared after the Spanish conquest, despite the terrible effect the conquest had had on the Indians. Whole portions of the population, which had never been exposed to common European diseases, died in the epidemics that arrived with the Spanish. Many of those who survived disease died as slaves as the result of brutal treatment they suffered in Spanish mines or on Spanish estates. Spanish priests converted Indians to Roman Catholicism, but they kept many of the rites and beliefs of their old religions. Despite everything, Indian culture persevered.

The Spanish ruled Mexico for 300 years, and during that period people of Spanish ancestry held nearly all power in the society. Indians continued to live in their villages and work the land much as they had done for centuries. They were joined by a growing number of *mestizos*, or people of mixed Spanish and Indian blood, who also became farmers, craftsmen, and laborers.

Mexico finally won its independence in 1821, after a long war with Spain. The country, which then extended into most of what is today the southwestern United States, continued to be ruled by a small minority of people primarily of Spanish descent. In 1836 Mexico lost Texas to American settlers who proclaimed their own republic, and in 1846 the United States, anxious to expand to the west, declared war on Mexico. Two years later the war ended in a complete U.S. victory, with Mexico forced to give up what is now Nevada, California, and Utah, as well as parts of Arizona, New Mexico, Colorado, and Wyoming.

General Antonio López de Santa Anna, who had led Mexico in the disastrous wars with Texas and the United States, was driven from power in 1855 by the Liberal party and its leader, Benito Juárez, a Zapotec Indian, who soon issued the famous reform laws. A civil war soon followed between the Liberals and the Conservatives; called the War of the Reform, it lasted from 1858 to 1861 and ended in victory for Juárez and the Liberals.

One year later, Spanish, French, and British troops occupied the Mexican port of Veracruz when Juárez stopped payments on Mexico's national debt. France attacked Mexico and the war of the French intervention was under way. French troops occupied Mexico City and in 1864 installed Maximilian, the brother of the Austrian emperor, as emperor of Mexico. But in 1867 the French were forced to withdraw, Juárez returned to power, and Maximilian was executed. Juárez died five years later, and in 1876 Porfirio Díaz seized power in a military coup. He was to remain in control of Mexico until the Mexican Revolution in 1911.

Maximilian, the French-installed emperor of Mexico from 1864 to 1867. In 1862, France, demanding the payment of debts, invaded Mexico, but five years later the war of the French intervention ended when the French withdrew. The reformer and Mexican leader Benito Juárez ordered Maximilian's execution.

As a child, Emiliano grew up in surroundings where the use of horses and guns was second nature. He enjoyed listening to the stories told by his uncles Christino and José, who had fought in the War of the Reform and against the French intervention in the 1860s; his Uncle José first taught him how to shoot a rifle and to hunt deer. Zapata's grandfather had fought against the Spanish in the War of Independence, and the villagers had battled bandits from the neighboring hills of the Puebla border. When he was not needed at home, Emiliano was sometimes sent to attend a local school, where the teacher was also a veteran of the war of the French intervention.

The village was a very old and tightly knit society with a tradition of elected village leaders, called *calpuleques*, and village councils that went back more than 400 years, to the time before the Spanish had conquered the Indians in Mexico. Members of the Zapata family had frequently occupied positions of leadership in these councils, and as Emiliano approached adulthood, he found a place for himself as a young but respected member of his village.

Zapata's village of Anenecuilco was located in the east-central portion of the fertile and extensively irrigated state of Morelos. The landscape of this state varies from the heavily wooded slopes of snow-capped volcanoes in the north, to the lush, almost tropical river valleys in the south, to the ranges of stony hills in the center. Just to the north of Morelos, on the other side of the volcanoes, lies Mexico City, the capital of Mexico.

Anenecuilco and the other villages of Morelos had existed for hundreds of years with a subsistence agriculture in which the villagers grew most of what they needed and had little contact with the outside world. In keeping with their inherited Indian traditions, much of the village land was owned and worked by the village community rather than by individuals. The village councils and older, more respected villagers made many of the agricultural decisions for the community, which grew primarily beans and corn and raised livestock.

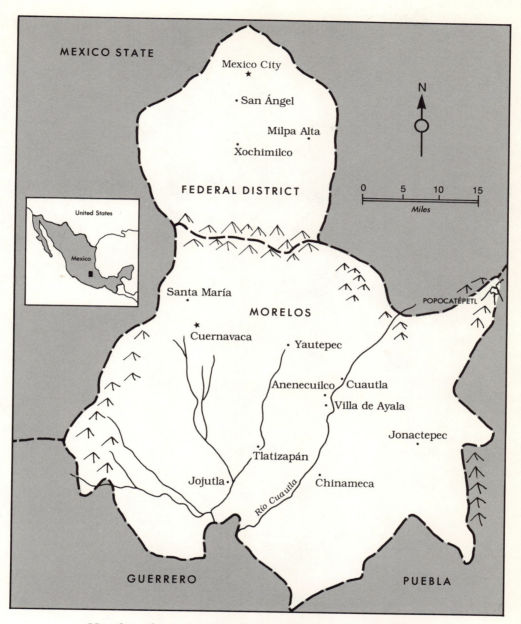

MEXICO STATE

Mexico City
★

• San Ángel

Milpa Alta
•

• Xochimilco

FEDERAL DISTRICT

N

United States

Mexico

0   5   10   15

Miles

Santa María
•

MORELOS

POPOCATÉPETL

★
• Cuernavaca

• Yautepec

Anenecuilco • Cuautla
•
• Villa de Ayala

Jonactepec
•

• Tlatizapán

Jojutla •

• Chinameca

Río Cuautla

GUERRERO

PUEBLA

Morelos, the second smallest of Mexico's 31 states, has a land area of 1,908 square miles (about the size of the U.S. state of Delaware) and borders on the Federal District that includes Mexico City, the national capital. Marked by many mountains, hills, and fertile river valleys, it is one of the nation's richest agricultural areas.

A train in the mountains of Morelos around 1900. The extension of U.S.- and European-owned rail lines into rural Mexico spurred the rapid growth of large-scale commercial agriculture. By 1910, Morelos had become one of the world's foremost sugar-producing areas.

There had been large haciendas and sugar plantations in Morelos before the Díaz regime came to power, but they had not been efficient, commercial enterprises; they were more like old-fashioned feudal estates. There were few railroads to ship sugar and other produce, the hacienda milling machinery was inefficient, and there was no large network of consumers ready to buy the sugar. Because of this, the haciendas did not expand rapidly or interfere with the security of the slow-moving, old-fashioned village way of life.

But with the arrival of the Díaz government, large-scale commercial agriculture appeared in Morelos. New, efficient milling machines were brought in to extract greater quantities of sugar from the sugarcane. Rail lines were extended into the state, allowing the sugar to be shipped out quickly and in larger amounts. The sugar plantations expanded rapidly; by 1908, Morelos was the world's third-greatest sugar-producing region, surpassed only by Hawaii and Puerto Rico. Fortunes were made and the sugar planters built great palaces, with fountains, palm trees, and enormous gardens, which stood in marked contrast to the increasing poverty of the surrounding Indian villages.

Morelos had developed what is called a "cash-crop economy," in which one large crop — in this case, sugarcane — was grown for export and sale on the world market. Everything in Morelos now depended on sugarcane, and a good year for sugar could produce enormous profits throughout the state. But a bad year — the result of a poor harvest or a drop in the price of sugar on the world market — could produce economic disaster. This meant that only large, efficient producers with the cash reserves to survive the shocks of a bad year could be successful. One by one, the smaller haciendas and independent ranches began to fail, leaving most of the land under the ownership of a handful of very powerful men.

The large hacienda owners bought out the smaller ranches and often acquired village lands by other means. Many bribed judges to have village land titles declared defective or to obtain favorable court rulings; quite often they would simply occupy the land with armed guards. With villages disappearing under the pressure of the expanding plantations, and the majority of the state's population being converted into dependent laborers and debt slaves, the sugarcane industry was destroying the traditional village society of Morelos.

Many villages in Morelos that tried to resist the takeovers were dealt with harshly. The village of Tequesquitengo was deliberately flooded after the villagers offended a nearby hacienda owner, who diverted the runoff from his irrigation system into their lake until only the spire of the village church showed above the water. Another hacienda owner took the opposite course with Tetelpa, simply cutting off its water supply. When Pablo Escandón, later governor of the state, fenced in 3,500 acres of communal pastureland belonging to the town of Yautepec, the townspeople sent a commission to President Díaz in Mexico City. Their documents were seized and the leader of the commission was last heard from on a prison train headed for a labor camp in Quintana Roo. Village leaders who opposed the hacienda owners fled to hideouts in the hills, only to find that the police imprisoned their families as hostages.

> *In time only [Tequesquitengo's] church spire remained above water, a reminder of the risks of independence.*
> —JOHN WOMACK, JR.
> American historian

Mexican peasants harvest a cactus plant. The expansion of haciendas to accommodate large-scale agricultural enterprises disrupted traditional rural life. Land used for generations by villagers to grow beans, corn, and other staple foods was taken over by the haciendas to grow more profitable export crops such as sugarcane.

The Díaz government was strongly in favor of the growing sugarcane industry. The regime considered Mexico's Indians — nearly 75 percent of the country's population — and their old-fashioned village system as obstacles to economic progress. During the last few years before the revolution, villages and small towns throughout Morelos declined in population and disappeared as their lands were expropriated and their economies pushed to the breaking point.

It was under these difficult circumstances that Emiliano Zapata grew up. This quiet boy with enormous, sad eyes had heavy responsibilities thrust on him at an early age. His mother and father died within nine months of each other when he was 16 years old. His father's last wish was that Emiliano should take care of his sisters, the house, and the family land. Emiliano's older brother, Eufemio, was given his share of the inheritance in cash and became a traveling peddler in Vera Cruz, although he returned frequently to Anenecuilco for visits. Emiliano's sisters were soon married, and he continued to work the family farm alone. He also raised horses and livestock and ran trains of pack mules down the Cuautla River valley in the off-season. Zapata sometimes sharecropped on hacienda land, dividing the yield 50–50 with the owner, but he did not work as a hacienda laborer. He was respected throughout the area for his skill as a horseman, and he sometimes trained horses for a local hacienda owner who was President Díaz's son-in-law.

After taking over the family farm, Zapata rapidly became involved in the growing conflict between the villagers and the haciendas. He sometimes lost livestock that had wandered onto pasture claimed by neighboring haciendas. The hacienda would then hold the livestock without feeding it until Zapata had paid a fine; at other times, the hacienda would keep one animal out of five and return the others.

Zapata was active in the *junta de la defensa*, or village defense committee, which tried to defend village lands, and he became known as someone who would stand up to the hacienda guards. At about the age of 18, he got into an argument and then a fight with some of the guards and was arrested by the rural police. As he was being led away, his brother Eufemio and a number of friends arrived on horseback and held the police at gunpoint. Eufemio cut the rope that bound Zapata; they and their friends rode away, and the rescue was complete. Emiliano and Eufemio then fled to the hills of Puebla state, where they worked for a year until the village elders straightened things out with the police so that they could return to Anenecuilco.

In 1909, the growing opposition to Díaz in Morelos ran its own candidate in the election for governor of the state. He was an old veteran of the war of the French intervention, General Francisco Leyva, and his campaign called for land and water for the villages. The candidate supported by the Díaz government was Pablo Escandón, the hacienda owner who had seized the communal pasture of the town of Yautepec. When an Escandón campaign train arrived in Cuautla it was greeted by a crowd of 1,500 people and shouts of "¡Viva Leyva!" One of the government speakers lost his temper and yelled back at the crowd, calling them "imbeciles" and "ungrateful bums." Rocks began to fly and first the rural police, then federal troops were called in. A number of the campaign leaders were deported to labor camps in the Yucatán. The Leyva campaign marked the beginning of the rebellion in Morelos.

Soon afterward, in September 1909, Zapata was elected calpuleque of the village council of Anenecuilco. He was barely 30 years old, and his election was a great honor for someone so young. Zapata's election also had another meaning. In times of war or trouble it was customary for the older men of the village council to retire in favor of the younger men, the "warriors" who were more capable of defending the village. The four old men who retired that day specifically recommended that they be replaced by younger men because Anenecuilco was in serious trouble: It was steadily losing land to the neighboring haciendas and its population was decreasing. The next calpuleque would have to vigorously defend the communal pastures, or the village itself might disappear.

Rocks sailed up toward [the government speaker] and the crowd turned into a nasty yelling mob. The rurales got ready to fire, and the people scattered in wild disorder.
—JOHN WOMACK, JR.
American historian

Strikers at the Rio Blanco textile plant in eastern Mexico in 1908, a few days before government troops broke the strike with much bloodshed. The events leading up to the outbreak of the Mexican Revolution were marked by a breakdown of central authority and labor unrest directed against the Díaz regime.

Zapata's first task was to examine the village land titles and maps. He and members of the village council went to Mexico City to hire a lawyer and to speak with Díaz's political opponents. The authorities in Morelos were not pleased, so they turned to a tactic frequently used in Mexico for controlling troublemakers: conscription into the army. In February 1910, Zapata was drafted and found himself a private in the Ninth Cavalry Regiment. But after just six weeks he was released, thanks to a request by President Díaz's son-in-law, the rich hacienda owner for whom Zapata had done some extra work training horses. In May, Zapata returned to his village of Anenecuilco to find that a neighboring hacienda had occupied much of the villagers' remaining land. Furious, Zapata organized a force of 80 armed villagers and occupied the disputed lands.

To the surprise of everyone in the area, the authorities did nothing in response to Zapata's move; they were worried about revolutionary activity elsewhere in the country and did not want to provoke an outbreak in Morelos. In fact, several court rulings favorable to the villagers were announced later in 1910, allowing them to remain on the land. Encouraged, members of the neighboring villages of Villa de Ayala and Moyotepec joined the Anenecuilco village defense committee. Zapata led the combined forces of all three villages in knocking down hacienda fences and occupying disputed lands to which the villagers claimed title. By the end of 1910, Zapata was leading such actions throughout the surrounding area. The police hesitated to interfere because the Ayala area, where the villagers had frequently organized vigilante groups to deal with bandits and had a long history of rebellion, was known as one of the most independent and heavily armed in the state.

Zapata used the respite to build the influence he would later wield as a guerrilla leader. He would turn out to be very different from most of the other leaders of the Mexican Revolution. He would always remain a small farmer, a villager, and a village council president. Later, when he controlled the entire state of Morelos, his government was little more than an armed association of the state's village and town councils, which he held together through a mixture of persuasion and respect.

Zapata loved village life in Morelos, with its horse races, cockfights, and rodeos, and he would always feel intensely uncomfortable in Mexico City. He did not set himself above his followers, and he never adopted a military uniform; to the last day of his revolt, he wore the *charro* clothes that a respected village leader would wear on a special occasion: enormous embroidered sombrero, short black jacket, boots, and tight-fitting Mexican trousers with lines of silver buttons down the side. Outsiders would laugh at these flamboyant clothes and note that the cloth was coarse and that the buttons were made of cheap silver. After seeing Zapata's sister dressed for a special occasion and wearing her old-fashioned jewelry, an American embassy official remarked that "everything she had on her person could probably have been purchased for about $5 American money."

But no peasant in Morelos ever saw Zapata and his officers without recognizing them instantly for what they were: respected village leaders such as they had known and followed all their life. Zapata, in turn, was completely loyal to the villagers of Morelos and to the village society from which he came. Unlike so many people fighting for power in Mexico at that time, he could not be bought and would not compromise on the one demand that meant everything to his followers: land reform. In this quiet man the villagers of Morelos had found a skillful and charismatic leader of great personal integrity, who inspired an almost religious devotion in the state's agricultural population.

What convinced them that once in power [Zapata] would not change and abuse their trust— what kept the question from rising in anyone's mind—was the reputation of his family.
—JOHN WOMACK, JR.
American historian

3

The Revolution Betrayed

Francisco Madero entered Mexico City on June 7, 1911, to the cheers of one of the largest crowds that the capital had ever seen. Over 100,000 people lined the boulevards of the city, waiting for a glimpse of the man who had overthrown Díaz. The largest earthquake in living memory had shaken the city the night before Madero's arrival, symbolizing for many the destruction of the Díaz regime and the violence of the revolution.

The beginning of the end for Díaz had come in 1908, when the 78-year-old president gave an interview to an American journalist and said that he would welcome democratic opposition. Many Mexicans took the statement seriously, even though it was meant only to please a foreign journalist. Within months Francisco Madero, the 35-year-old son of a large landowner from northern Mexico, published a book called *The Presidential Succession* in which he criticized the Díaz government and called for democratic elections.

Madero accomplished the overthrow of Díaz in ten months of planning and action. It was a victory won, too soon.
—JOHN WOMACK, JR.
American historian

Francisco Madero arrived in Mexico City in June 1911, two weeks after Díaz stepped down from the presidency and fled the country. Madero had been jailed in 1910 for opposing Díaz in an election but escaped to the United States and served as the revolutionaries' political leader.

A park in a wealthy section of Mexico City. Díaz lost the support of the middle classes by filling high-ranking jobs with foreigners. University-trained Mexicans found few job opportunities upon graduating and abandoned the dictator for Madero.

The following year saw the outbreak of rebellion in the north and south, and in 1910 Madero ran openly for president against Díaz. Madero was promptly jailed and Díaz was reelected, but soon thereafter Madero escaped from prison and fled to the United States. From just across the border in Texas, he continued to organize opposition to Díaz.

Throughout Mexico, the political situation was deteriorating for Díaz. The urban, educated upper-middle class was turning against him; there were so many foreign experts working in the country that even university-educated Mexicans, the sons of the urban middle class, could not find jobs. The press, too, turned against the dictator, as American and Mexican writers published scathing articles and books about debt slavery in rural Mexico.

In March 1911, Madero returned to Mexico, providing Zapata and his fellow revolutionary leaders with their cue to start the revolt. It did not take long for Díaz to see that the situation was hopeless; he resigned on May 25 and fled the country. Two weeks later Madero arrived in Mexico City.

One of the first to greet Madero as he stepped off his train was Emiliano Zapata. It was only three months since Zapata and his villagers had broken into the police station at Villa de Ayala and ridden down the Cuautla River valley, but now Zapata was one of the most important rebel generals in southern Mexico. The two men shook hands, Zapata in his colorful charro outfit and Madero, a small man with a pointed beard, in his politician's black suit and tie.

Zapata and Madero came from very different backgrounds. While Zapata was a villager of modest means and only the most basic education, Madero had grown up wealthy and attended universities in California and in Europe. Madero was a sincere, idealistic man who believed in democracy but did not want the large-scale land reform that would fundamentally change the structure of rural Mexico. He did, however, support a more moderate program of reform and had promised to restore to the Indian villagers the lands which the haciendas had "arbitrarily" and "in such an immoral way" taken from them.

Zapata's support for Madero during the revolution was based on this pledge. But in the treaty that ended this phase of the revolution, Madero, not wishing to antagonize the landowners, had compromised on the issue, merely urging the state governments to study the possibility of land reform. Furthermore, he believed — naively as it would turn out — that the federal army Díaz had created would now obey the new government; thus Madero agreed to disband the revolutionary armies that had brought him to power. It was already clear that the revolution did not mean the same thing to Madero that it did to Zapata.

The two men met for lunch at Madero's house in Mexico City, Zapata dressed as always in his charro clothes, carrying his rifle, and wearing an enormous sombrero. He found himself in an elegant Mexico City dining room, surrounded by the kind of people he had fought against all his life: politicians and hacienda owners in black suits and ties.

Madero tried to persuade Zapata and his rebels to disband and trust him. His efforts fell through when the interim government launched military operations against them; they dug in and fought.
—CHARLES C. CUMBERLAND
American historian

Southern rebels pose for a photo in 1911. Upon becoming president, Madero agreed to disband the rebel forces so that the federal army could reestablish order. Initially reluctant, Zapata agreed to disarm all but 400 of his troops; shortly thereafter Madero demanded that the number be reduced to 50 men.

After the meal, according to Zapata aide Gildardo Magaña, Madero explained to Zapata that it was important to begin disarming the revolutionary troops and sending them home, as Mexico was now at peace. Zapata replied that he did not trust the federal army. Furthermore, he continued, "What interests us is that, right away, the lands be returned to the villages and the promises which the revolution made be carried out." Madero replied that this was a complicated problem that would take a long time to solve.

Zapata stood up and walked over to Madero with his rifle, which he had kept beside him throughout the lunch, and said that in the state of Morelos "a few hacienda owners have taken over by force the lands belonging to the villages. My soldiers, the armed farmers and the people of the villages demand that I tell you, with all due respect, that they want the restitution of their lands to begin right now."

Zapata then invited Madero to visit Morelos and inspect the situation himself. Madero replied that he was sure that everything would be arranged satisfactorily and told Zapata that "in recognition of the services you have rendered to the Revolution, I am going to see that you are properly rewarded by being able to acquire a nice ranch."

Zapata slammed the butt of his rifle violently into the floor and said angrily, "Señor Madero, I did not join the Revolution in order to become a hacienda owner; if I am worth anything, it is because of the confidence and the trust which the farmers have in me. Well, they believe that we are going to fulfill the promises that we have made to them and if we abandon these people who have made the Revolution, they will have every right to turn their guns on those who have forgotten their promises."

Zapata reiterated the villagers' demand that their land be returned to them, and Madero smiled and promised to come to Morelos and see conditions there himself. Zapata then returned to the train station with his escort of armed Morelos villagers to take the train back to Cuernavaca.

Long before his interview with Madero, Zapata had already taken steps in Morelos to implement the revolutionary program as he conceived it. After taking Cuautla on May 19, 1911, he had ordered the villagers throughout the area to tear down the hacienda fences and to reoccupy the lands that the hacienda owners had taken from them. He also sent detachments of his troops to help the villagers in case they encountered any resistance. The hacienda owners were furious. Much of the best land was now occupied by armed villagers, who began to plant beans and corn, not sugarcane. A local agrarian party was growing around Zapata; the village councils were vigorously asserting themselves. The villagers themselves no longer came to work on the haciendas, listened submissively to the hacienda owners, or obeyed the hacienda guards. There was talk of appointing Zapata governor or police chief of the state. To the hacienda owners, all of this constituted a tremendously alarming threat.

> *The Morelos movement settled into permanent rebellion under its own banner, the Plan de Ayala, which branded Madero a traitor and charted a land-reform program.*
> —CHARLES C. CUMBERLAND
> American historian

Citizens of El Paso, Texas, stand atop freight cars to get a better look at the fighting just across the Rio Grande in Ciudad Juárez, Mexico, on May 10, 1911, during the first pitched battle of the Mexican Revolution. Within three weeks, Díaz resigned, fled the country, and Madero returned to assume the presidency.

But nothing frightened them more than the way that waves of Zapata's poorly armed peasants had overwhelmed the well-trained troops and machine guns of the Cuautla garrison. If all the peasants started to behave like that, there would not be enough soldiers in Mexico to keep them down. Zapata was described in the conservative press as a modern Attila, an enemy of the better classes, and a primitive Indian villager who would destroy civilization in Morelos.

Now, with the revolution seemingly over and Madero organizing the government in Mexico City, it was necessary to appoint new governors in the states. In Morelos, the government's choice was Juan Carreón, the manager of the Bank of Morelos and a strong supporter of the hacienda owners — a sign that Madero preferred to appease the large landowners rather than the peasants. Nevertheless, as Zapata returned from Mexico City, he still had faith in Madero's sincerity and hoped to convince him of the need for land reform when Madero came to visit Morelos.

Madero arrived in Cuernavaca on June 12, 1911, and stepped off the train to the cheers of an enormous crowd. A double row of Zapata's troops lined the street from the station to the center of town, and Zapata and his officers escorted Madero's carriage through the crowd, first on foot, then on horseback. Madero, accompanied by a group of Morelos businessmen, went directly to an elegant banquet given by Juan Carreón, the governor. The guest list was almost exclusively made up of hacienda owners, businessmen, and former Díaz supporters. Zapata arrived late because, as he put it, he refused to dine with enemies of the revolution; he arrived only after the banquet was over.

Later Madero reviewed Zapata's troops. Rosa King, an Englishwoman who owned a hotel in Cuernavaca, wrote a vivid account of the parade:

> Surely all the strength of the Zapatistas was kept for action, for they wasted none on uniforms or martial drill. Poor fellows, in their huge straw hats and white cotton "calzones" [coarse cotton trousers and shirts], with cotton socks in purple, pink or green pulled outside and over the trouser legs. They were equipped with rifles of all sorts, and one poor little cannon. But even the cannon looked proud of being a follower of the brave leader, Emiliano Zapata. Among the troops were women soldiers, some of them officers. One, wearing a bright pink ribbon around her waist with a nice big bow tied in back, was especially conspicuous. . . .

My soldiers—the armed farmers and all the people in the villages—demand that I tell you, with full respect, that they want the restitution of their lands to be got underway right now.
—EMILIANO ZAPATA
to Madero

The presence of women officers and soldiers was so unusual that it attracted a great deal of attention. But the spectators soon saw this woman appear again and again:

> It gave the game away, for it was soon seen by that vivid bit of color that the troops were merely marching around a few squares and appearing and reappearing before Don Francisco Madero. The pathetic attempt to please Madero by seeming stronger in numbers than they were was funny, but it was sad, too. Behind that sham was indomitable spirit. Mr. Madero's face, far from expressing any consciousness of the amazing reappearance of the same "battalions" in such quick succession, was perfectly impassive.

Madero spent most of the remainder of his visit with the hacienda owners. He promised to name Zapata chief of the federal police in Morelos, but he would not endorse further land reform and ordered Zapata to disband all but 400 of his troops immediately.

General Victoriano Huerta in Cuernavaca, the capital of Morelos. In the late summer of 1911, after conservative supporters of the hacienda owners gained the upper hand in the central government, Huerta led the federal army into Morelos to capture Zapata and stop peasant reoccupation of disputed lands.

Zapata's troops began to turn in their arms on June 13, 1911. Each veteran surrendered his gun and passed before a table, at which sat Zapata, his chief of staff Abrahám Martínez, and Madero's representative Gabriel Robles Domínguez. Zapata knew most of the troops personally; he thanked each one and signed their discharge papers. They were given 10, 15, or 20 pesos apiece depending on how much money they needed to get home and how many guns they turned in. After the process was completed, Robles Domínguez told Zapata that he was authorized to give him as much money as Zapata wanted. The general thanked Robles Domínguez, refused, then looked over at a group of widows who had lost their husbands in the recent fighting. "Please give me 500 pesos," he said. Taking the money he walked over to the women, gave it to them, and said, "Let these poor people at least get this."

In the next few days Zapata received a telegram confirming his appointment as police chief, but on June 19 Governor Carreón refused Zapata 500 rifles he had requested to arm his police force. Zapata was then called to Mexico City where Madero told him that because of tremendous opposition from the hacienda owners, he could not appoint him police chief after all. He would have to retire to his village, where he would be allowed to keep a personal escort of 50 men.

Zapata accepted what seemed to be the end of his political career. In an interview with a newspaper reporter he explained that he had joined the revolution not because he needed money. He also said that he was looking forward to going back to his little farm in Morelos. On his return to Anenecuilco he made plans to marry Josefa Espejo, a woman from nearby Villa de Ayala, and settled back into life in his village.

In spite of Zapata's retirement, the hacienda owners found that they could not reassert their control over Morelos. Every village in the state was now filled with bragging, unsubmissive veterans of Zapata's campaigns. Village councils throughout the state began meeting publicly, demanding their lands back from the haciendas, and bringing out old deeds dating back to the Spanish conquest of Mexico. Large sections of the haciendas were occupied by villagers squatting on disputed land. Most important of all, these villagers were now heavily armed. Angry accusations were made that when the Zapatistas had surrendered their arms they had kept their best rifles and given up old, useless ones instead.

Meanwhile, in Mexico City an intense political battle was developing. Madero had hoped to unify the country by providing open elections supervised by a bipartisan provisional government, made up of a balanced blend of former Díaz supporters and supporters of Madero. To guarantee that the elections would be impartial, Madero did not take part in the provisional government. Its president was Francisco León de la Barra, who had been foreign minister under Díaz. But the minister of the interior, who controlled the federal police, was Emilio Vásquez Gómez, one of Madero's men.

The caretaker government did not unify the country as Madero had hoped. Instead, it was soon split by a power struggle between the conservative former supporters of Díaz and the more radical of Madero's supporters. Emilio Vásquez Gómez was one of Madero's most radical adherents, and he began to send secret shipments of guns to the Zapatistas. Vásquez Gómez, who had always sympathized with Zapata's ideas of agrarian reform, feared a conservative military takeover of the government. In case fighting broke out again, he wanted to see the radical Zapatistas prevail.

Some revolutionary troops had also been kept in government service, including a Zapatista detachment in Puebla state whose commander was Abrahám Martínez, Zapata's chief of staff. On July 12, 1911, Martinez arrested several conservative legislators suspected of plotting to kill Madero. The prisoners were rescued by federal troops in a pitched battle which left at least 50 Zapatistas dead and Martínez a prisoner.

Zapata immediately remobilized his entire army and sent telegrams to Madero and Vásquez Gómez saying that if they were in danger he was ready to

> *Put Zapata in his place for us, since we can no longer stand him.*
> —FRANCISCO MADERO
> to the military commander
> in Morelos

43

march, and that he awaited their orders. Madero replied that Zapata should stay where he was; later he issued a public statement praising the federal troops for restoring order. Zapata and his men were angry and felt betrayed. They wanted concessions and guarantees from Madero before they would agree to demobilize again.

President de la Barra and the rest of the conservatives in the provisional government refused to negotiate with Zapata and his villagers. On August 2, 1911, Zapata's ally Vásquez Gómez was relieved of his duties as minister of the interior and replaced by Alberto García Granados, whose policy with respect to Zapata was that "the government does not deal with bandits." Zapata, meanwhile, was back in Anenecuilco, occupied with his wedding to Josefa Espejo. The civil ceremony had taken place in June, but the religious ceremony was set for August, and the two families were in the middle of wedding celebrations when a messenger arrived with news that a large body of federal troops under General Victoriano Huerta had entered the state.

Madero rushed to Morelos to head off the fighting, but as he was not a member of the provisional government his only power was his great personal prestige as leader of the revolution. He praised Zapata as his "truest general," and the two men quickly worked out what they considered to be a satisfactory agreement. Madero cabled the results to President de la Barra, who grudgingly accepted them but continued to send ambiguous orders to General Huerta. Zapata once again began to demobilize his men, but the federal troops continued to advance, despite the agreement. Madero sent frantic telegrams to Mexico City demanding that the troops be halted, but to no avail. It was clear that the conservatives in the federal government wanted to crush Zapata.

A number of Madero's men were sure that Madero had betrayed them; the American historian Roger Parkinson describes Zapata's brother, Eufemio, as wanting to shoot "the little squirt." Instead, Zapata escorted Madero to the Cuautla station and put him on a train, telling him, according to Gildardo Magaña, to "go to Mexico City, Señor Madero, and leave

It is truly objectionable, that an individual of [Zapata's] antecedants, whose actions make us fear new outrages, be allowed to maintain [that] attitude you are familiar with.
—LEÓN DE LA BARRA
to Madero

us here. We'll deal with the federal troops." Referring to the approaching presidential elections, which Madero was expected to win, Zapata added, "We will see how you fulfill your promises when you come to power."

With the advancing federal troops only two miles outside of Cuautla, Zapata evacuated the town and ordered his remaining forces to disperse into the countryside. Zapata sent a last telegram to Mexico City stating that he had complied with the agreement and was not in revolt against the provisional government. The next night he was nearly caught by a surprise attack at the Chinameca Hacienda, where he had tried to get a few hours' sleep, and had to jump out the back window in the middle of the night and run for his life through the sugarcane fields. A few days later, Zapata was a solitary refugee in the mountains of Puebla.

Zapatista soldiers, wearing the traditional white outfit of the southern Mexican peasant, in the Morelos countryside. Zapata's forces were excellent guerrilla fighters who could quickly disperse when outnumbered by government soldiers and regroup elsewhere.

4

The Triumph of Force

While Zapata was lying low in the mountains of Puebla, General Victoriano Huerta embarked upon a campaign of brutal repression in Morelos. By August 27, 60 people in northern Morelos had been executed by Huerta's troops. Within a few days they had spread out across the state, shooting scores of suspected rebels and forcibly moving thousands of villagers into centrally located labor camps. According to the American historian John Womack, Jr., Huerta wrote cynically to President de la Barra that "with the rifles and the cannon of the Government of the Republic," he was "preaching harmony, peace, and brotherhood among all of the sons of Morelos." Huerta's offensive forced thousands of villagers to flee into the mountains. There they joined Zapata, who had linked up with some of his troops.

The Morelos campaign . . . is what technically is called a campaign of occupation.
—VICTORIANO HUERTA

Two heavily armed military doctors attached to Huerta's federal army pose for the camera in the Morelos town of Yautepec in 1911. With Zapata and his forces hiding in the hills, Huerta occupied the state in a brutal campaign designed to crush the peasant movement.

Morelos peasants confined behind barbed wire in 1911. Huerta and his successor as commander of government forces in Morelos, Juvencio Robles, ordered all villagers to assemble in camps where they could be controlled by the army. Robles also ordered the burning of villages to break the peasant movement.

One month after Huerta's invasion, Zapata was ready to make his move. On September 26, 1911, the same day Huerta reported to de la Barra that the state had been "pacified," the federal government received an angry petition from Zapata demanding the withdrawal of all federal forces from Morelos and the implementation of land reform. At the bottom of the text, perhaps intentionally, was written the date and place of issue: San Juan del Rio, a remote village in the mountains of southern Puebla. Within hours, Huerta received orders from the president to march on the village and capture Zapata. Huerta set out immediately with most of his troops.

The Zapatistas were indeed there, but they fell back as Huerta advanced, drawing him deeper and deeper into the mountains, until Zapata suddenly slipped around his flank with a small force of several hundred men and charged back into Morelos, just in time for the presidential elections of October 1, 1911. With Huerta still bogged down in the mountains, much of the state rose in revolt again as Zapata once more rode through the Cuautla River valley. By October 22, he had crossed the northern border of the state and occupied villages only 15 miles from the center of Mexico City. Panic swept through the capital, the legislature went into permanent session, three cabinet ministers were replaced, and Huerta was fired.

Madero, meanwhile, had been elected president by an overwhelming majority. As he awaited his inauguration, which was set for November 6, 1911, Madero issued a statement in which he said that it was the fault of de la Barra's government that Zapata was in revolt. Madero added that Zapata and he had agreed on the conditions necessary for ending the revolt in Morelos, and that after the inauguration these conditions would be fulfilled. Even Zapata had expressed faith in Madero's sincerity, saying only that he doubted that Madero had the practical ability to fulfill his promises. As a gesture of good faith, Zapata withdrew his forces from the Mexico City area and assembled them around Villa de Ayala to await negotiations with Madero.

On November 8, 1911, two days after Madero's inauguration, an envoy from the new president arrived in Cuautla. He was Gabriel Robles Domínguez, with whom Zapata had already worked during the first demobilization of Zapata's troops in Cuernavaca. The two men quickly and easily reached an agreement, which included a guarantee of agrarian reform, the appointment of 500 of Zapata's men as rural police under the command of Madero's brother, the withdrawal of federal troops from the state, and Zapata's retirement to his village. While they were talking, however, the federal army once again closed in, surrounding Villa de Ayala. When Robles Domínguez tried to return to Mexico City to speak with Madero, the federal commander would not let him leave.

Robles Domínguez cabled Mexico City, telling Madero that he and Zapata had reached an agreement and that Madero must stop the army immediately. The next day Robles Domínguez evaded the federal troops and got to Mexico City, only to find that the president once again felt that he had to compromise. Madero said he would accept nothing less than Zapata's surrender to the federal troops. In return he guaranteed that Zapata would not be harmed and would be allowed to live in exile in another part of Mexico.

Hurrying back to Cuautla, Robles Domínguez found the federal army preparing to attack Zapata the next day. The envoy was unable to get through the cordon to see Zapata, but the next morning he was able to send a hastily written note assuring Zapata that he would be safe if he surrendered. Zapata received the letter, along with Madero's official demand for his surrender, on horseback as he watched federal troops take up positions less than a mile away. He calmly organized a rearguard action and ordered most of his troops to retreat to the hills and disperse.

That night Zapata slipped through the federal lines to retreat once again to the mountains of Puebla. Again Madero sent commissioners to negotiate with the elusive rebel. When they finally found him, according to John Womack, Zapata told them angrily:

> Madero has betrayed me as well as my army, the people of Morelos, and the whole nation . . . nobody trusts him any longer because he's violated all his promises. He's the most fickle, vacillating man I've ever known. . . . Tell him this for me: to take off for Havana, because if not he can count the days as they go by, and in a month I'll be in Mexico City with 20,000 men, and have the pleasure of going up to Chapultepec Castle and dragging him out of there and hanging him from one of the highest trees in the park.

On November 28, 1911, Zapata issued his famous Plan of Ayala from a mountain stronghold in the state of Puebla. "The immense majority of the com-

Let Zapata know that the only thing I can accept is that he immediately surrender unconditionally and that all his soldiers immediately lay down their arms.
—FRANCISCO MADERO

mon people and citizens of Mexico," it said, "own no more than the land on which they walk, suffering the horrors of miserable poverty without being able to better their social condition in any way nor to dedicate themselves to industry of agriculture because the lands, timber, and water are monopolized in a few hands." It called on all villagers whose lands had been illegally seized by the haciendas to take up arms immediately and reoccupy those lands by force, whatever the cost. Angrily and emotionally, it called for the overthrow of Madero's government, declaring that he was a traitor who had not kept his promises and had betrayed the principles of the revolution. The Plan of Ayala was a fervent, unpolished document in a language and style that any Morelos villager could understand. Written by Zapata and Otilio Montaño, the schoolteacher at Villa de Ayala, and typed by a village priest on a battered old typewriter, it was an appeal that would set the Mexican countryside on fire.

Government troops led by General Felipe Ángeles (with goggles) await orders in May 1912. Madero removed Robles from command of the federal army in Morelos and replaced him with Ángeles, who ended the army violence against the civilian population. The Zapatistas, however, continued to burn the haciendas' sugarcane fields.

When a Mexico City newspaper editor went to Madero and asked if he could publish the Plan, Madero told him to go ahead, so everyone could see how crazy Zapata was. But Madero had completely misjudged the importance of the Plan of Ayala. The newspaper published a double edition that day, which sold out almost immediately. The demand for copies of the Plan was so great that another special edition had to be published the following day. Within two months, agrarian revolts had broken out over a five-state area in southern Mexico as armed villagers swarmed over the haciendas, reoccupying land and stubbornly defending every foot of it against the army, the rural police, and the hacienda guards.

In Morelos, Zapata's close friend and ally Genevevo de la O began systematically blowing up military trains coming into the state from Mexico City. De la O was a Morelos villager and charcoal maker who wore the same coarse white shirt, loose pants, and big sombrero as the peasants he had led since the outbreak of the revolution almost two years before. Now recognized as a rebel general second in stature only to Zapata himself, de la O controlled the rail lines that ran past his village of Santa María and soon had a stranglehold on Cuernavaca as well. As his forces laid seige to the state capital in February 1912, federal troops retaliated by storming de la O's village of Santa María, dousing the houses with kerosene, and burning the whole village to the ground. De la O's daughter was among the villagers killed in the fire.

In an attempt to end the revolt, Madero appointed General Juvencio Robles commander of the federal army in Morelos. Robles (no relation to Robles Domínguez) had gained a reputation for toughness in the Indian wars in northern Mexico, and he lived up to that reputation upon taking over in Morelos. He methodically marched on the state's agricultural villages and burned them, either "resettling" the villagers in concentration camps near the main towns, or shipping them off to labor camps in the Yucatán. Rosa King described a prison train full of villagers leaving Cuernavaca as follows: "The soldiers were

> *All Morelos . . . is Zapatista, and there's not a single inhabitant who doesn't believe in the false doctrines of the bandit Emiliano Zapata.*
> —JUVENCIO ROBLES

52

hustling the poor wretches into a cattle box car, pushing them in till there was not even standing room. They boarded up the doors and nailed them shut . . . I had seen in the car an Indian who had worked for me for four or five years, faithfully, and I began to protest very bitterly. . . . 'Now, now señora,' replied General Robles, who was inspecting the train, 'you must not take it so hard. You are only a woman and you do not understand these things. Why, I am trying to clean up your beautiful Morelos for you. What a nice place it will be once we get rid of the Morelenses [inhabitants of Morelos]! If they resist me, I shall hang them like earrings to the trees.' "

Armed Zapatistas taken prisoner in battle by Robles's forces were generally hanged on the spot, and King wrote of their shriveled corpses swinging from trees throughout the state. "Zapata's men not only fought," she wrote, "they had, in between, to work to provide for their families, cultivating their patches of corn and beans . . . many of these men were surrounded by the Federals while thus working unprotected in the fields. They were made prisoners and driven to the nearest towns, where they were forced to dig their own graves before they were shot — if one can call 'graves' the holes into which their bodies were thrown."

The American industrialist Meyer Guggenheim and his sons. The Guggenheims owned mining operations throughout Mexico, and in some Mexican states their companies were exempt from paying taxes. Many U.S. capitalists, anxious to preserve their business interests in Mexico, opposed the revolutionaries.

The American newspaper magnate William Randolph Hearst, a supporter of Mexican conservatives, had large investments in Mexican cattle and sugarcane. In 1915, Hearst's papers — which in 1898 had successfully urged the United States to declare war on Spain — called for "the planting of the [U.S.] flag all the way to the Panama Canal."

Robles's brutal tactics only succeeded in arousing intense hatred for the federal army among the state's peasants. Zapata was swamped with recruits, and in March 1912, Pascual Orozco led a revolt in northern Mexico, further complicating the situation for the federal army. By April the Zapatistas controlled large parts of the Morelos countryside, where they imposed a weekly tax on the haciendas and set a minimum wage for hacienda laborers; haciendas that did not comply had their fields of sugarcane burned.

But by May 1912, the rebels were running out of ammunition, which they could only obtain by attacking and capturing federal camps and supply trains. Orozco's revolt in the north was also in trouble. The spring planting season had started and many of Zapata's men returned home to their farms. A bloody stalemate had developed in which the federal troops controlled the towns and cities while the Zapatistas controlled the countryside.

Madero tried to break the stalemate in Morelos by replacing Robles with a new commander, General Felipe Ángeles. A French-trained former director of Mexico's National Military Academy with a reputation as an honorable man and a brilliant field commander, Ángeles was of Indian descent and likelier to initiate a more sympathetic policy toward the Zapatistas. Ángeles immediately stopped the indiscriminate burning of villages and killing of civilians. He allowed Zapata's sister, mother-in-law, and sisters-in-law, who had been taken hostage by Robles, to return home. Ángeles continued to use large forces to aggressively pursue the rebels, but he also made it clear that no questions would be asked of Zapatistas who left the revolt and returned to their villages to work their fields in peace.

Ángeles, Madero, the state government in Cuernavaca, and the national government in Mexico City all began to work on modest land reform plans. The fighting subsided as the peasants, tired of warfare and bloodshed, returned to their villages. It was during this period that Zapata and Genevevo de la O later said they had the greatest difficulty in keeping their men together and the most serious doubts about their rebellion.

The hacienda owners, however, wanted more vigorous action against the Zapatistas. They continued to lose fields of sugarcane, which were burned when they did not pay the tax imposed by the rebels; by January 1913, more than 50 percent of the state's cane fields had been destroyed. The hacienda owners were further angered when it was announced that Madero's minister of development was studying the possibility of breaking up the large haciendas.

Discontent with Madero's government was also strong among foreigners with large investments in Mexico: the British, Spanish, Germans, and particularly the Americans. The 1890s and early 1900s was a period of financial expansion for the industrialized nations, prompting the construction of railroads and the establishment of steamship lines throughout the world. These made it possible to transport large quantities of bulky agricultural

> *[Angeles] was . . . deeply ambitious, but had the political sense to advance his career subtly and always in seeming modesty.*
> —JOHN WOMACK, JR.
> American historian

United States ambassador to Mexico Henry Lane Wilson was a strong supporter of U.S. business interests in Mexico — and a strong opponent of Madero's. In February 1913, he welcomed the armed overthrow of the Madero government by conservative elements of the Mexican army.

goods over great distances at very low prices. Large-scale commercial agriculture and mining in countries with cheap labor, such as Mexico, became very profitable for American and European investors, because these goods could now be shipped and sold anywhere in the world. United States investment in foreign countries mushroomed, particularly in Mexico, Central America, and the Caribbean.

By 1900, American and European corporations had gained control of the economies of a number of Latin American countries, with U.S. military might following closely to "protect American interests," as it was put by U.S. politicians and journalists. In 1903 U.S. warships forced Colombia to recognize the independence of Panama so that the U.S.–owned Panama Canal could be completed; invaded the Dominican Republic in 1904 when that country failed to meet its debts; occupied Nicaragua in 1911 to prevent the Europeans from building a competitor to the Panama Canal; and repeatedly took over the Cuban government from 1906 to 1912 to allow American-owned sugar plantations to operate unfettered by local laws.

In Mexico, U.S. companies and other foreign interests controlled the economy. More than 75 percent of Mexico's mining industry was owned by two American companies, Guggenheim and U.S. Smelting, and the oil industry was controlled by the Waters-Pierce Oil Company, Standard Oil, and the Dutch Shell Oil Company. Americans such as William Randolph Hearst had made enormous investments in the cattle and sugarcane industries. Now, with disruptions caused by the revolution, these investors were losing money on their Mexican enterprises. Many hoped for the reappearance of another strongman like Díaz to reimpose order in the country and guarantee a return to the cheap labor and trouble-free work environment of the Díaz period. Investors who had money in haciendas and agricultural industries like sugarcane were often in favor of expanding the haciendas and were strongly opposed to agrarian reform movements like Zapata's. President Madero was seen as too weak, and his plans for breaking up the large estates and limiting foreign control of Mexico were dangerous to foreign investment. One of the biggest complaints against Madero was, in the words of the historian Friedrich Katz, that "he had been either unable or unwilling to suppress Zapata."

Under the Republican administration of U.S. president William Howard Taft, the United States had been a strong supporter of Díaz. "I am glad to aid him," Taft wrote to his wife in 1909, "for the reasons that we have two billions of American capital in Mexico that will be greatly endangered if Díaz were to die and his government go to pieces. . . . I can only hope and pray that his demise does not come until I am out of office. . . ." Taft's ambassador to Mexico was Henry Lane Wilson, a Wall Street corporate lawyer who was strongly supported by the American business community in Mexico.

Bodies lie in a street in Mexico City in February 1913 during the 10 days of fighting that marked the overthrow of Madero's government. General Ángeles and his forces backed Madero but were defeated by troops loyal to Huerta and other conservative officers. Madero was captured and held prisoner.

Madero (right) and his vice-president José Pino Suarez (left) at a 1911 peace conference. After they were captured in the coup of February 1913, both the new president, General Huerta, and U.S. ambassador Wilson refused to intercede on their behalf despite appeals from around the world. They were shot on February 22.

After the fall of Díaz, Ambassador Wilson repeatedly warned the Mexican government that the United States would not tolerate damage to American property. He characterized Zapata and his supporters as "savages" and believed that Madero was both unable to reimpose order in Mexico and too hostile to American business. The ambassador publicly opposed Madero in a series of diplomatic showdowns in 1911 and by late 1912, according to a dispatch sent by the German minister to his government, Ambassador Wilson had proposed that the United States overthrow Madero and intervene militarily in Mexico. By early 1913, Ambassador Wilson had established close contact with a number of federal army officers who were hostile to Madero.

On February 9, 1913, a revolt against Madero broke out in Mexico City. General Felipe Ángeles quickly returned to the capital with most of his troops to aid the president, but after 10 days of fighting, Madero's government was overthrown by a group of conservative military officers. There were hundreds of civilian casualties and many atrocities. Madero's brother Gustavo, who led Madero's party in the National Assembly, was captured by a group of soldiers who gouged out his one good eye before bayoneting him to death.

Ambassador Wilson gave Washington advance notice of the coup the day before it happened. Only hours after Madero was captured, the leaders of the coup met at the U.S. embassy. With American warships standing off the coast and U.S. forces mobilized on the Mexican border, the coup leaders agreed on the formation of a new government and were introduced to the diplomatic community by Ambassador Wilson at a champagne buffet. "Mexico has been saved," announced the U.S. ambassador in an emotional speech. "From now on we shall have peace, progress, and prosperity."

Madero, his vice-president Pino Suarez, and General Felipe Ángeles were held prisoner in the National Palace. Appeals came in from around the world to spare their lives. Mrs. Madero went to the embassy to beg Ambassador Wilson to intercede for her husband. According to the American historian and journalist Ernest Gruening, the ambassador refused, telling her curtly, "Your husband's downfall is due to the fact he never wanted to consult with me." He called Pino Suarez "a very bad man [to whom] I cannot give any assurance of his safety. . . . That kind of man must disappear."

During the last hours of his life, Madero spoke about Zapata with General Ángeles, who was later freed. Zapata had been right, Madero told Ángeles, when he argued that the federal army could not be trusted. Madero had believed that the army would obey a democratically elected president, but he had been wrong.

On the night of February 22, 1913, Madero and Pino Suarez were taken behind the central prison and "shot while trying to escape."

> *When the cannons finally quieted on February 19, Madero . . . had resigned, and Huerta . . . emerged as caretaker president.*
> —JOHN WOMACK, JR.
> American historian

5

A Fight to the Death

The federal army was now openly in power in Mexico. The new president was General Victoriano Huerta, the ruthless commander who had ravaged Morelos in August and September of 1911 before being outmaneuvered by Zapata in the mountains of Puebla. Francisco León de la Barra, the former president of the federal government and foreign minister under Díaz, was now vice-president, and Alberto García Granados, who had refused to deal with "bandits" like Zapata, was once again minister of the interior. These were Zapata's worst enemies, and the Zapatista agrarian reform was exactly the kind of thing they wanted to stop at all costs. Behind these men stood the Mexican federal army, for a long time an independent force in Mexican politics but usually allied to the large landowners. In the past, the army had most frequently used its guns not against foreign enemies but against Mexicans, putting down peasant and Indian revolts as it protected property and imposed order on the countryside.

[Huerta] aggravated turmoil into a terrible crisis, and Mexico moved into a profound social revolution.
—JOHN WOMACK, JR.
American historian

Pancho Villa riding alongside a column of his army in the northern state of Chihuahua in 1914. Villa had strongly backed the late Madero and vowed to overthrow the military government of General Huerta.

Victoriano Huerta, who became Mexico's president in February 1913, with members of his cabinet. The new U.S. president, Woodrow Wilson, refused to recognize Huerta's "government of butchers" and authorized the sale of arms to the northern rebels.

Now, unrestrained by a civilian government, the army could attack Zapata with impunity. General Juvencio Robles was once again appointed military commander in Morelos, with orders to stamp out the Zapatista rebellion there by whatever means necessary. Operations began in April 1913, when Robles arrived in Cuernavaca. Within two days he had arrested a number of state legislators and shipped them off to prison in Mexico City. He then declared himself governor of Morelos and ordered all rural residents of the state to leave their houses and concentrate in army-controlled towns by May 16; after that date, anyone caught in the countryside without a pass would be shot. As the peasants arrived in the towns many of them were either drafted into the army or deported to labor camps. Columns of federal troops crisscrossed the state, burning villages and looking for rebels.

Many of the villagers did not report to the towns, fleeing instead to the hills to join Zapata. His forces grew, but his biggest problem was getting guns and ammunition. Nearly every weapon Zapata's men acquired was taken from the federal troops or from federal supply trains. When he captured Jonacatepec, for example, Zapata got 2 machine guns, 330 carbines, 310 horses and saddles, and hundreds of prisoners, including 47 federal officers, whom he released. "You and your men are set free," Zapata told the federal commander of the town. According to Gildardo Magaña, Zapata said:

> You are pardoned and your lives are spared on the sole condition that you do not take up arms again against the Revolution. Tell your chief Huerta, that the "bandits" of the south, as he calls us, set their prisoners of war free, while he and his men who call themselves the "constituted government" assassinate revolutionaries. Tell him also to send me more soldiers, because I need arms. We will take their guns away from them too.

The astonished federal commander later joined Zapata and became one of his most important contacts for buying guns and ammunition smuggled out of federal army supply depots.

A street in a northern Mexican town after an attack by the federal army. Huerta ordered government forces to renew their offensive against the rebels both in the north and in Morelos, where all civilians found outside army-controlled towns were ordered to be shot.

Zapatista forces were accompanied by large numbers of unarmed peasants called "buzzards," who wanted to join them but did not have guns. At the end of every battle they rushed onto the field, stripping the dead soldiers of their guns and ammunition. Deserters from the federal army also provided arms. Most federal soldiers were peasant conscripts who did not want to be in the army. To prevent their deserting to the enemy, men drafted in northern Mexico were usually sent to southern Mexico to fight, and conscripts from the south were sent north so that they would not be familiar with the local people. Nevertheless, hundreds of soldiers deserted to the Zapatistas, who were peasants like themselves. The deserters gave the Zapatistas rifles and ammunition in return for enough food and money to get home. Some joined the rebels. The Zapatistas gave common soldiers who had been taken prisoner the same options, but captured federal officers who had burned villages or executed prisoners were shot.

Emiliano Zapata (seated, center) and his brother, Eufemio (seated, left), among their men in 1914. Zapata ordered that captured government soldiers be set free if they surrendered their arms and promised to return to their homes. In contrast, captured Zapatistas were usually killed by federal troops.

A 1928 photo of Álvaro Obregón, commander of one of three northern rebel armies of 1913. A rancher, teacher, and inventor of agricultural machinery, Obregón was a moderate who favored labor and agrarian reforms and who was an advocate of Indian rights. He was elected president in 1920.

Zapata was careful to retain the allegiance of the local villages. "When asking for food," he ordered his men, "you will do so with good words, and whatever you want, ask for it in a good manner, and always show your gratitude." Instructions issued to his officers and troops during this period strictly forbade pillage, robbery, or drunken and disorderly conduct in the towns; furthermore, they were to help local villages reoccupy lands taken from them by the hacienda owners. The Zapatistas continued to finance their revolution by "taxing" the haciendas, burning them and their fields of sugarcane if they did not pay.

By August 1913, a stalemate had once again developed in Morelos, with Robles's federal forces holding the towns, and the Zapatistas the countryside. Meanwhile in the north, Venustiano Carranza, Pancho Villa, and Álvaro Obregón had risen against Huerta in the freewheeling style of northern Mexico, commandeering trains and roaring across the great northern deserts with armies of soldiers, their wives, their children, and their horses all packed into and atop hundreds of boxcars.

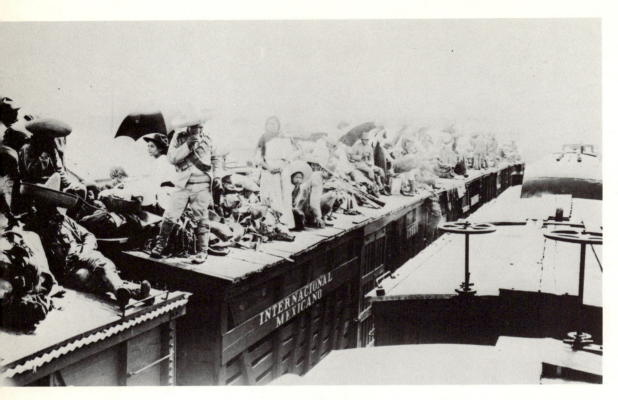

Villa's rebel army often rode from place to place, and even into battle, packed into and atop freight cars. Ironically, the rail lines had been built to transport minerals and agricultural products from U.S.- and European-owned mines and plantations — the very thing many of the rebels were fighting against.

Pancho Villa was the wildest and most colorful of the northern leaders. A bandit and cattle rustler who first joined the revolution because the Díaz government had put a price on his head, Villa had been devoted to Madero and cried openly at memorial services for the dead president. Violent and emotional, he attracted an army of thousands through the force of his magnetic personality and dynamic leadership. He was often at the head of his troops, throwing dynamite bombs and leading wild charges. Using heavily armed trains like tanks, he would come charging into towns garrisoned with unsuspecting federal troops, smashing their defenses. Villa and the other northern revolutionaries were heavily armed because they had easy access to weapons brought across the border from the United States. Nearly everyone fought in the battles: 12-year-old children covered with bandoliers of cartridges and carrying carbines were a common sight, as were women, some of whom served as officers.

Álvaro Obregón was a more moderate man, a mechanic, rancher, schoolteacher, and construction contractor from a small town in northern Mexico. He was a strong advocate of better working conditions for rural and construction laborers, and he himself had worked at many different trades and was the inventor and builder of agricultural machinery particularly suited to conditions in northern Mexico. Practical and extremely intelligent, he became one of the most skillful generals of the Mexican Revolution. Obregón had grown up in close contact with the Mayo and Yaqui Indian tribes and spoke both the Mayo and Yaqui languages. These Indians now formed the backbone of his army.

Venustiano Carranza, the third northern leader, was a representative of the large landowners. He had been a senator under Díaz but had supported Madero because he saw the need for reform, although like Madero he did not want the reforms to go too far. Madero had appointed him governor of the state of Coahuila, and after Madero was overthrown, Carranza refused to recognize Huerta's military government. Though not a particularly effective general, Carranza was an excellent politician, and with the support of the Coahuila state legislature he had gained political control of the revolution in the north, where he proclaimed himself "First Chief of the Revolution."

The bearded Venustiano Carranza, the third northern rebel leader, sits with his staff during a lull in the fighting. As governor of the state of Coahuila, Carranza was one of Madero's more conservative supporters. In March 1913, he revolted against Huerta and proclaimed himself "First Chief of the Revolution."

U.S. president Woodrow Wilson, who in April 1914 ordered U.S. forces to occupy the Mexican port of Veracruz. Wilson acted in part to prevent the entry of a German ship carrying arms intended for the Huerta government.

By September 1913, the three northern rebels had established control in the region, forcing Huerta to withdraw most of his troops from Morelos to fight in the north. He left only enough soldiers in the state to hold the major towns. Zapata, meanwhile, moved most of his forces south into the neighboring state of Guerrero, making alliances with the local revolutionary chiefs there, and took Chilpancingo, the state capital of Guerrero, on March 23, 1914. By now the Zapatista agrarian revolt had spread to a five-state area in southern Mexico. Strengthened by his success at Chilpancingo, where he had captured large quantities of arms and ammunition, Zapata turned back toward Morelos to attack the few towns there that remained under federal control.

The Huerta regime, buffeted by military defeats at home, was also in trouble on the international front. Two weeks after the coup in which Huerta came to power, a new president was inaugurated in the United States, the Democrat Woodrow Wilson (no relation to Ambassador Henry Lane Wilson).

President Wilson intended to pursue a new, more "moral" foreign policy. "Usurpations like that of General Huerta," said his secretary of state, William Jennings Bryan, "menace the peace and development of America as nothing else could. If General Huerta does not retire by force of circumstances, it will become the duty of the United States to use less peaceful means to put him out."

In Mexico City, Ambassador Wilson sent several cables to Washington, urging the United States to recognize the Huerta regime, but President Wilson refused. "I will not recognize a government of butchers," he said before firing Ambassador Wilson. He then approved the sale of arms to the northern rebels. When asked by a British diplomat what he hoped to accomplish with his Mexican policy, President Wilson's grandiose reply was: "I am going to teach the South American republics to elect good men!"

A landing party from a U.S. warship in the Veracruz harbor heads for shore two days after the April 1914 bombardment and occupation of the port, in which 200 Mexican defenders were killed. President Wilson was surprised when the Mexican rebels joined Huerta in condemning the U.S. action.

Obregón (third from left) meets with Villa (in hat, to the right of the tent pole) in August 1914, one month after rebel gains and the U.S. occupation of Veracruz led Huerta to resign and flee the country. While Obregón, Carranza, and Villa vied for control of Mexico, Zapata was content to limit his concerns to Morelos and its vicinity.

In April 1914, several sailors from American warships off Mexico's east coast went ashore to load gasoline in Tampico; another group of sailors landed to go to the post office in Veracruz, Mexico's largest port on the Gulf of Mexico. In both cases they were detained by the Mexican authorities for a few hours before being released. The American admiral demanded that the Mexicans apologize and "publicly hoist the American flag in a prominent position on the shore and salute it with 21 guns." The Mexicans refused. A few days later President Wilson received word that a German steamship was nearing Veracruz with a large cargo of arms and ammunition for Huerta. Using the post office incident as a pretext, Wilson ordered the navy to occupy Veracruz and prevent the ship from making its delivery.

The American attack on Veracruz took place the next day, April 21, 1914; 200 Mexican soldiers, 21 American sailors and marines, and an undetermined number of civilians were killed before the Americans took the city. War fever swept the United

States: The newspaper chain owned by William Randolph Hearst, who had large investments in Mexico and Central America, soon called for the "planting [of] the American flag all the way to the Panama Canal." But to Wilson's surprise, Mexicans of all political persuasions were united in outrage against the American attack. Both Huerta and Zapata angrily denounced it, and in the north Carranza officially protested "the invasion of our territory."

But while Huerta evacuated government forces from Morelos to prepare defenses against the Americans, Zapata moved in to take over the towns the federal troops had abandoned. And despite all their public pronouncements of outrage at the invasion, neither Zapata nor any of the other revolutionaries agreed to join with Huerta to fight the Americans.

The situation for the Huerta regime steadily deteriorated. On July 15, 1914, Huerta resigned and fled the country on the same German steamship that had taken Porfirio Díaz into exile four years before. Huerta left behind a caretaker government, which desperately tried to negotiate with the revolutionary forces advancing on Mexico City.

The Zapatistas wanted more than the ouster of Huerta; they demanded the removal of the entire government and its replacement by a government dedicated to the principles of agrarian reform. On July 19, Zapata's forces captured the town of Milpa Alta in the southern suburbs of Mexico City. At night their campfires could be seen from the capital, covering the slopes of the volcanoes to the south. But the Zapatistas still did not have enough ammunition for a major attack on the city.

The caretaker government held on desperately for another month, until they could negotiate an agreement with Carranza, the most conservative of the northern revolutionaries. On August 13, 1914, troops loyal to Carranza occupied Mexico City and replaced the federal troops in the city's southern defensive positions, to prevent the Zapatistas from entering the capital. Once again, Zapata and his villagers had been frozen out of any real political power.

While Mexicans Cut Gringo Pigs' Throats, In the Churches the Gloria Rings Out.
—headline from *El Independiente* after the American invasion at Veracruz

6

Morelos Comes into Its Own

In the late summer and early fall of 1914, Zapata and his forces held the countryside and the mountains just south of Mexico City. Carranza and his troops were dug in opposite them in the capital itself. The two men tried to work out a settlement and head off a renewal of the fighting, but according to Gildardo Magaña, Carranza insisted that any settlement depended on the recognition of his authority. "Tell Zapata what my proposal is," Carranza had said to the first Zapatista envoys, "and if he does not accept it I have 70,000 rifles to make him submit. . . . Don't forget that I am the First Chief."

Carranza, a wealthy and experienced politician, found it difficult to deal with a person of Zapata's social class. According to Magaña, Carranza's reaction to Zapata's first written settlement proposal was disdainful "when he saw Zapata, a clodhopper, a Mr. Nobody, expressing his ideas to him with hot truth and with absolute critical independence. It is an error to judge a document by the social extraction of the person who signs it, but that is what he did."

[Carranza is] glutting himself with his triumphs.
—EMILIANO ZAPATA

Villa, in the president's chair, and Zapata, in the vice-president's, sit side by side in the National Palace in Mexico City in December 1914, shortly after they had met for the first time. The alliance between the two revolutionaries fell apart within weeks.

Venustiano Carranza, the most conservative of the three northern revolutionaries, took over the central government in August 1913 after Huerta fled Mexico. The Zapatistas feared that Carranza, whom Zapata called "that son of a bitch," would wipe out the agrarian reforms they had achieved in Morelos.

Zapata and the villagers of Morelos, on the other hand, feared a new betrayal of their agrarian principles at the hands of national politicians like Carranza. They knew how strong and persistent the hacienda system was in Mexico. Zapata hated Mexico City, which he called a "nest of politicians and a focus of intrigues," and when Carranza proposed that Zapata come there to meet him, Zapata replied that Carranza should instead come and meet him in Morelos. "This business of dividing up the land is crazy," Carranza told two of Genevevo de la O's representatives, explaining that he could not accept the Plan of Ayala. As contacts continued between the two leaders, the tone heated up. The Zapatistas were "bandits without a flag," said Carranza, who insisted that they must submit unconditionally to his government. The negotiations finally broke down for good on September 5, 1914.

A few days later, Carranza called for a convention of revolutionary leaders, hoping they would ratify his position in power. Zapata was interested in this convention because he knew that although most of the revolutionary leaders had accepted Carranza's authority, some of them, like Pancho Villa, were seeking to break away. Others, like Álvaro Obregón, wanted the convention to bring an end to the war by establishing a government that all of the revolutionaries could accept. Obregón and the moderates saw Carranza's inflexible and authoritarian attitude as an obstacle to peace. They also believed that the convention would have to include the Zapatistas. For his part, Zapata knew that an assembly of revolutionary leaders would be more sympathetic to his agrarian reforms than Carranza was.

The convention opened in Mexico City on October 1, 1914, without the participation of the Zapatistas. However, the delegates soon established their independence from Carranza by moving the talks north to the town of Aguascalientes and invited the Zapatistas to send a delegation. As Zapata's representatives entered the theater where the convention was being held, the delegates applauded wildly, pounded their rifle butts on the floor, and fired pistol shots into the ceiling. A measure supporting Zapatista principles of agrarian reform as set forth in the Plan of Ayala was approved soon thereafter.

Pancho Villa soon emerged as Carranza's chief rival for power when the convention delegates declared themselves the sovereign government of Mexico and dismissed Carranza as First Chief. The delegates appointed an interim president who would prepare the country for elections. Carranza refused to recognize the convention's decision, prompting Villa to mobilize his troops for a drive on Mexico City in November 1914. Obregón and many of the moderates abandoned the convention and sided with Carranza when they saw that Villa had gained control, preferring the politician's authoritarianism to the bandit leader's wildness. The Zapatistas, on the other hand, stuck with Villa and the convention, which was the only group in Mexico willing to recognize their principles of agrarian reform.

The only basis of peace which the revolutionaries of the south admit is . . . the absolute submission of the Constitutionalists to the Plan of Ayala in all its parts.
—MANUEL PALAFOX
Zapatista minister
of agriculture

In late November 1914, as Villa drove down from the north, Carranza withdrew his forces from Mexico City to the port of Veracruz, recently evacuated by the United States. Since Villa's forces had not yet reached the capital, it was the Zapatistas who moved in and occupied Mexico City on November 24, 1914. These rugged country soldiers in their rough peasant clothes and enormous sombreros were awed by and uncomfortable in the big city. When they were hungry they knocked on doors and asked for tortillas and other country food, refusing unfamiliar white bread. Some of them went into Sanborn's, one of the most elegant establishments in the city, and had their pictures taken while having coffee at the breakfast counter. Their appearance was terrifying. They were dirty, unshaven, and loaded down with guns and cartridge belts.

Delegates to the Aguascalientes convention of October 1914. Carranza organized the conference to end the fighting and affirm his authority, but the delegates rejected him, invited the previously ostracized Zapatistas to participate, and declared themselves in charge of Mexico pending new elections.

All of Mexico City feared the Zapatistas would embark on a rampage of burning and looting. For years the conservative press had published stories about Zapatista "atrocities"; Zapata had been called the Attila of the South and his army portrayed as an uncontrollable mob of rioting, burning, pillaging peasants — even though the reports of Zapatista "atrocities" were consistently contradicted by eye-witnesses who reported that when Zapatista troops occupied a town, there was no such behavior. And as it turned out in Mexico City, the Zapatista forces committed little, if any, violence against the civilian populace or property. Nevertheless, to middle- and upper-class Mexicans the spectacle of hordes of Morelos peasants forming armies, defeating federal troops, and capturing the capital seemed to shake the foundations of their society.

Uncertain of their role [in Mexico City, the Zapatistas] did not sack or plunder, but like lost children wandered through the streets knocking on doors and asking for food.
—JOHN WOMACK, JR.
American historian

Villa (in general's uniform) mobilized his forces against Carranza in November 1914 after the Aguascalientes convention delegates rejected Carranza's claim to the Mexican presidency. Zapata supported Villa and the convention's endorsement of agrarian reform; Obregón, who did not trust Villa and wished to see an end to the war, backed Carranza.

Zapata, who did not like Mexico City any more than his troops did, stayed for two days in a grimy little hotel by the railway station. As soon as Villa's troops began to arrive, Zapata returned to Morelos, without even waiting to speak with Villa. His troops also returned to Morelos as soon as they were replaced at their posts by Villa's men. Zapata, as always, was happy to leave the national government to others if they, in turn, would leave him alone in Morelos.

Zapata's return to Morelos worried Villa, who needed Zapata to continue the campaign against Carranza. Although Villa and Zapata had never met, there had already been frequent contact between their movements. Villa had spent months in prison with Zapata's aide Gildardo Magaña, who had given the northerner a clear idea of what the Zapatistas were fighting for. Magaña had also taught Villa how to read.

Both Zapata and Villa came from the poorly educated lower classes of Mexican society and they felt keenly the limits imposed by their lack of education. Villa complained that when he signed an order, he never knew if he was signing his own death sentence. Under Magaña's instruction, he had eagerly devoured a history of Mexico and gone on to read parts of *Don Quixote* before escaping from prison. Because they both came from Mexico's impoverished rural population, Villa and Zapata felt an instinctive sympathy for each other, and they both understood the importance of land reform for Mexico's peasants.

The two leaders finally met on December 4, 1914, in the little village of Xochimilco, about 12 miles south of Mexico City. Villa arrived on horseback with a small cavalry escort and was met by villagers and schoolchildren singing songs and carrying bouquets of flowers. Villa and his men could not carry all the flowers which were pressed upon them, and hundreds of the blossoms fell to the ground carpeting the road as Villa passed through the brightly decorated village to the schoolhouse where Zapata was waiting. The room where they began their meeting was packed with people; besides Zapata's staff, there were local village leaders, Zapata's sister, his little son Nicholas — who slept through most of the meeting — an observer from the U.S. embassy, and all the curious villagers who could squeeze into the school. Zapata and Villa had little to say at first as they sized each other up, but they soon found themselves agreeing about Carranza. "I always told them Carranza is a son of a bitch," said Zapata. "Those are men who have always slept on soft pillows. How could they ever be friends of the people, who have spent their whole lives in nothing but suffering?" Zapata had cognac served and toasted their friendship, but Villa, who never drank alcohol, choked and coughed when he tried to down his glass. Taking him by the arm, Zapata led him to a quieter room. There the two men talked for an hour and a half, agreeing on a joint drive toward Carranza's forces in Veracruz. Villa would attack from the north, and Zapata would come in from the south through the

Carranza's soldiers strike a dramatic pose in this 1914 photo. With Villa's and Zapata's armies closing in on Mexico City in November of that year, Carranza's forces abandoned the capital and regrouped in the Gulf of Mexico port of Veracruz, from which the Americans had recently withdrawn.

city of Puebla, which was strategically located halfway between Veracruz and Mexico City. Villa promised to supply guns and ammunition for the campaign and both leaders agreed to hold a joint review of their armies on December 6, 1914, in Mexico City.

Thousands of Zapata's and Villa's men marched through the streets of Mexico City two days later. Dressed in charro outfits, white work clothes, and big sombreros, they were a colorful sight. Villa wore a brilliant blue and gold uniform and had his picture taken in the presidential chair. Zapata was sitting beside him, looking suspicious and uncomfortable as he always did when he was in Mexico City.

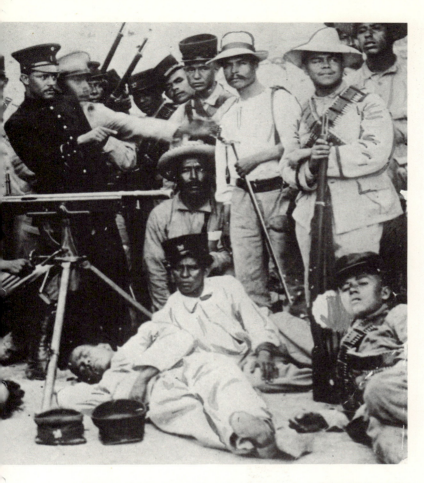

Eight days later the Zapatistas took Puebla city, but the alliance between the two leaders was already crumbling. Although Villa himself may have been sympathetic to the Zapatista concern with land reform, his movement was fundamentally different from Zapata's. Unlike the peasant farmers of Zapata's army, Villa's men were more often cowboys, used to the highly mobile life on horseback characteristic of northern Mexico. Coordination between the two armies was difficult, and most of the guns and ammunition that Villa had promised for the attack on Puebla had not arrived. Fighting had broken out in Mexico City between Zapata's and Villa's men, and Zapata's chief delegate to the convention had been shot and killed.

Zapata's chief delegate to the Aguascalientes convention, Paulino Martínez (seated second from left), among a group of Zapatista leaders in 1914. Martínez was killed when fighting broke out in Mexico City between Zapata's and Villa's men as the alliance between the two rebel leaders broke down.

Zapata's troops were tired of the seemingly endless fighting, first against the succession of conservative governments, and now against their fellow rebels. They had won their state of Morelos, occupied Mexico City, and captured Puebla, a city which to many of them seemed far away. Now they wanted to go home. It was harvest time and their crops needed work. Zapata shared this feeling with his men, his primary concern being local rather than national in scope. Leaving only a few troops to hold Puebla — and thus freeing Carranza's forces to concentrate on their battle with Villa in the north — he returned to Morelos to live in Tlaltizapán, a cool town full of green laurel trees that was located in the central part of the state. From this headquarters he organized what had always interested him the most, land reform in Morelos.

The Zapatistas' land reform program in the state was already under way. On September 8, 1914, Zapata had ordered the seizure of all the lands and urban property of those who opposed the Zapatista revolution, in accordance with the Plan of Ayala. These lands were distributed to the villages, and income from the urban property was used to provide pensions for widows and orphans of Zapatistas killed in the revolution and to establish credit institutions for small farmers. Now, in January 1915, the Zapatistas brought 41 young surveyors from Mexico City's National School of Agriculture to Morelos to clearly mark and record the boundaries of every village in the state. Using maps and records dating back hundreds of years, the surveyors reestablished the lands to which each village had a traditional and hereditary claim.

Morelos refugees during the revolution. The constant fighting cost thousands of lives and disrupted rural society for almost a decade.

During a lull in the fighting in Morelos in 1914–15, the Zapatistas passed the Agrarian Law, the most sweeping agrarian-reform law in Mexican history. The law upheld the rights of villages to hold communal lands and the rights of small farmers to work family holdings.

Nine months later, the Zapatistas passed the Agrarian Law of October 26, 1915. Effective throughout the state of Morelos, it was the most radical land reform law Mexico had ever seen. It set a maximum size for all farms in the state, depending on the kind and quality of the land involved. For example, a single farmer could not own more than 247 acres of the best-quality irrigated land, but he could hold as many as 2,471 acres of poor-quality land. The owner was compensated for any excess land taken by the government, which then redistributed it to landless peasants or villages. If redistributed to a village, it remained forever the property of that village. Land given to an individual farmer had to be cultivated by that farmer or his family, and if it was left idle for more than two consecutive years it reverted to the state for redistribution.

Manuel Palafox, the Zapatista minister of agriculture, was given the power to set up agricultural courts, agricultural banks, irrigation and farm construction services, as well as agriculture and forestry experimental stations. He also regulated water usage, mandating that agricultural uses took legal precedence over all other uses. "The nation recognizes the indisputable right," said the Agrarian Law, "of every Mexican to possess and to cultivate an area of land . . . sufficient to permit him to satisfy his needs and those of his family."

The harvest of autumn 1915 was one of the best the state had ever reaped. The farmers went back to growing corn, beans, chili peppers, onions, and other staple foods, which were now abundant and available throughout Morelos at lower prices than before the revolution. The state was finally at peace, with Zapatista troops guarding the mountain passes and roads at the border. Judge Duval West, who visited Tlaltizapán on a fact-finding mission for U.S. president Woodrow Wilson, reported that the peasants of Morelos saw Zapata "as a savior and as a father." According to the American historian Roger Parkinson, West found Zapata "friendly" but "concerned only with the situation within the state boundaries of Morelos." West believed that Zapata's politics were "naive"; for example, "Zapata saw no need for a rigid government or standing army: Instead, all men should carry arms as they worked their village fields, and if the enemy should come, then the men would turn upon them and drive them away." This, thought Zapata, was how the revolution had been won in Morelos, so "let the rest of Mexico secure its freedom and happiness in the same way."

Morelos was governed by a vigorous local democracy of village councils. When Zapata was called upon to settle a dispute, he inevitably ratified the decision of the local village council, or mediated between two village councils seeking compromise. Zapata even refused to organize a state police, because he felt that local law enforcement should instead be organized in each village by the local village council.

[The] repartition of lands will be carried out in conformity with the customs and usages of each pueblo.
—MANUEL PALAFOX
Zapatista minister
of agriculture

Troops loyal to Carranza display weapons captured from Villa's army in 1915. In the autumn of that year Carranza and Obregón forced Villa to retreat to the U.S. border and forced Zapata to withdraw from the Federal District into Morelos. Carranza's victories left him the recognized leader of Mexico.

Genevevo de la O was elected provisional governor by the Zapatista chiefs, and regular elections were scheduled to fill municipal offices and to elect state judges and a state legislature. When the Zapatistas wrote their Agrarian Law, they argued endlessly over whether land given to the villagers should be held and worked communally by the village in the traditional Indian style, or should be individually owned. Zapata's solution was to let each village decide for itself how its land would be held. Life in Morelos began to settle into the old contented rhythm of markets, bullfights, and warm evenings in the village plazas like that of Tlaltizapán, where Zapata and his chiefs drank beer and talked with local farmers about crops and the weather.

While Morelos enjoyed its first period of peace in five years, Carranza steadily regained control of the

rest of Mexico. His forces had reoccupied Puebla on January 4, 1915, only weeks after Zapata's forces had left the city. In the north, Obregón, the moderate who had reluctantly joined Carranza rather than Villa, defeated Villa in a series of battles in April and June of 1915. In one of the engagements Obregón lost his arm in a grenade blast and nearly died, but the war in the north was already won for Carranza.

As Villa's army retreated in disorder, Zapata brought many of his troops out of Morelos and tried to defend Mexico City, but Carranza's more heavily armed forces soon pushed the Zapatistas out of the capital. In October 1915, the United States recognized Carranza as the ruler of Mexico. Now firmly in control, Carranza was prepared to attack the Zapatista revolution in Morelos.

7

The Death of a Leader

By December 1915, Carranza had massed 30,000 federal troops on the borders of Morelos. The fighting began in early January 1916, but Carranza's federal forces were not able to break into Morelos until March, when a disgruntled Zapatista leader allowed Carranza's general, Pablo González, to enter the state through a mountain pass.

Genevevo de la O was able to slow down González's troops, but he could not stop them. They took Cuernavaca on May 2, 1916 — Zapata, who had arrived to organize the city's defense, barely escaped in time — and moved on through the state, routing the Zapatista forces. Within days of Cuernavaca's fall, González and the other federal commanders took almost all of the state's major towns, and once again the government army treated the civilian population with extreme brutality. On May 8, in the town of Jiutepec, they rounded up and shot 225 people. When González's troops took Zapata's headquarters at Tlaltizapán on June 10 they executed 132 men, 112 women, and 42 children. By the end of May about 1,500 people had been sent to labor camps in Yucatán.

> [González,] like the high politicians and generals of the new regime, was impatient to end the southern problem.
> —JOHN WOMACK, JR.
> American historian

Soldiers of Pancho Villa's Death Brigade in a northern Mexico stronghold in 1917. As the Mexican Revolution moved into its seventh year, fighting among the revolutionaries themselves became common. A number of Zapata's men were killed during factional fights within Zapatista ranks.

Northern rebels in Chihuahua state during the revolution's middle stages. A large number of the revolutionary fighters were boys under the age of 13.

The federal troops stole cattle, burned crops, and dismantled milling machinery to sell it as scrap iron. Groups of hundreds of people at a time were held for ransom and shot if they could not produce the sums of money demanded of them. Before the advancing troops, thousands of villagers fled south to the mountains, where Zapata and his chiefs, defeated in pitched battles, prepared a new approach.

Zapata regrouped his army into small guerrilla units of 100 to 200 men and in July launched a series of small attacks throughout the state. The Zapatista guerrillas successfully ambushed government patrols, and destroyed federal outposts and garrisons, slipping afterward into the villages to avoid detection. Knowing that the Zapatistas were being sheltered everywhere by the villagers, González turned to a tactic Robles had used three years before. He ordered all rural residents to abandon their villages on September 15, 1916, and to concentrate in the major towns where the army could more easily control them. Zapata countered with a series of decrees reaffirming village rights and ordering his troops to resist government efforts to remove villagers. The villagers, who regarded Zapata as their champion with an almost religious devotion, for the most part defied the government order and stayed where they were or fled to the mountains.

On October 4, 1916, a Zapatista force of 1,000 men struck to the north and captured the pumping station at Xochimilco, which supplied water to Mexico City. A week later they assaulted San Ángel, a suburb less than eight miles from downtown Mexico City. Other dramatic attacks were effected throughout a seven-state area in southern Mexico, all concentrating on lines of communication and other highly visible targets. The attacks were designed to discredit Carranza on the international scene by showing that he did not control the country.

One of the most effective attacks came on November 7, 1916. While González was in Mexico City discussing his campaign against the Zapatistas with the government, the whole city heard the boom of an explosion and the crackle of distant gunfire. The Zapatistas had blown up a train on Mount Ajusco, just south of Mexico City. More than 400 people were killed, and the smoke from the wreckage was clearly visible from the capital. González, enraged and terribly embarrassed, decreed that from then on, "Anyone . . . who directly or indirectly lends service to Zapatismo . . . will be shot by a firing squad with no more requirements than identification." According to John Womack, he also ordered an immediate death penalty for "anyone caught on the roads or paths without certified safe-conducts from . . . headquarters in Cuernavaca; anyone near railroad right-of-ways without satisfactory explanation; anyone not resettled in the specified towns; anyone who had given his personal safe-conduct pass to another; and anyone who had vouched for someone dishonestly requesting a safe-conduct pass." Within days the Zapatistas blew up another train on the same mountain.

[The Zapatistas are] barbarians . . . loathsome satyrs [of] bestial instincts, . . . felons and cowards by nature.
—PABLO GONZÁLEZ

By the end of November 1916, Zapata's army had retaken the initiative in Morelos, helped by an epidemic of dysentery that struck more than 7,000 of González's troops who had eaten large quantities of mangoes from the town markets. On December 1, 1916, Zapata launched simultaneous attacks against garrisons throughout the state. Within two months the Zapatistas had retaken Morelos and secured its borders.

For Zapata it was another dramatic comeback from the brink of defeat. But the year of warfare between his forces and Carranza's government army had devastated Morelos, a state that had already been ravaged repeatedly over the previous five years, to an unprecedented extent. An American observer compared it to the destruction he had witnessed in Europe, where World War I was raging. Famine spread through the state as the traditional village structure came close to disintegrating. Although Zapata tried to remedy the situation with new laws and the establishment of schools throughout the state, Morelos was still crippled.

The Zapatista leaders now turned on each other. Otilio Montaño, the schoolteacher who had helped Zapata to write the Plan of Ayala, became involved in a factional fight which led to revolt against Zapatista headquarters. He was tried and executed. As discipline broke down, another Zapatista commander shot 30 prisoners outright. In June 1917, Zapata's brother, Eufemio, loyal but wild and alcoholic, was shot and killed by one of his subordinates after he beat the man's father in a drunken rage. Zapatista commanders took advantage of an amnesty offered by Carranza and went over to the government side. Zapata himself became depressed and irritable, perhaps wondering if all the deaths and destruction were worth it.

Under these difficult circumstances Gildardo Magaña became increasingly important at Zapatista headquarters. A solid, peaceful man with quiet confidence, he was above all a skillful negotiator who sought a reasonable compromise wherever one was possible. He advised Zapata to look for allies among

92

other Mexican revolutionary movements and even in Carranza's government, so that the Zapatista movement would not remain isolated in Morelos. Zapata agreed and asked Magaña to negotiate on his behalf and to make contacts with other revolutionary leaders.

It was not an easy task. One meeting with a Zapatista chief, who had accepted amnesty from Carranza, developed into an angry shouting match that ended when the chief drew his pistol, fired point blank at Magaña, and missed. The 60 men at that meeting opened fire on each other as Magaña and the other leader rolled on the floor in a knife fight. Magaña escaped unharmed but the other leader was killed. Magaña continued the very touchy business of making contacts within Carranza's camp, paying particular attention to Álvaro Obregón, the northern moderate, who was now unhappy with Carranza's inflexible and authoritarian attitude.

U.S. Marines in El Valle, Mexico, in 1916. In early 1916, Villa raided the town of Columbus, New Mexico, killing 16 Americans. The raid prompted the marines, under General John Pershing, to pursue Villa's forces into Mexico, but after nine futile months Pershing withdrew with Villa still at large.

Gildardo Magaña, one of Zapata's closest aides, served as governor of the Federal District from March to June 1915, when the Zapatistas held control of Mexico City. Magaña later wrote a history of the Zapatista revolution that contains many eyewitness accounts of Zapata's personality, actions, and speeches.

In November 1917, Carranza's forces began a new offensive into Morelos. They took Cuautla but could go no farther, stopped by fierce Zapatista resistance. Fighting continued through the winter, and in February 1918 Zapata tentatively proposed to Carranza that if he would leave the Zapatistas in control of Morelos, they would recognize his authority as president of Mexico. Carranza did not reply.

Open warfare raged once again throughout the state. The harvests of 1918 were disastrous, and in October the deadly influenza epidemic that swept through the Western Hemisphere hit Morelos's hungry and malnourished rural population. In November Carranza's forces, once again under the command of Pablo González, pushed into the state. By February 1919, González controlled every major town in Morelos except for Tlaltizapán, where Zapata had his headquarters. The situation for Zapata was desperate, but he remained at large. No peasant or villager would turn him in.

Zapata's continued survival was embarrassing for Carranza. It implied to foreign governments that Carranza's government was not yet in full control of Mexico. Several of Zapata's remaining generals urged him not to risk military action, but to hide and wait until the national situation was more favorable.

Zapata's revolution seemed to have reached a dead end. Morelos was a wasteland. About 45 percent of the state's population was gone — killed, deported, dead of starvation and disease, or simply refugees in other parts of Mexico. The gutted and burned-out shells of the villages, which Zapata had sought to preserve, dotted the countryside. The traditional village society with its village councils had practically disintegrated. The war had destroyed the effects of Zapata's agrarian reform of 1915, and his previous alliances in national politics with Madero and Villa had failed.

The wreckage of a dynamited train outside Mexico City. One of Zapata's chief allies, Genevevo de la O, specialized in blowing up trains carrying government troops and supplies. Like Zapata, de la O was a villager from rural Morelos.

Eufemio Zapata poses in a retouched photograph shortly before his death in 1917; he was killed by a man whose father Eufemio had beaten in a drunken rage. With Carranza's forces defeating Zapata in Morelos and Zapatista fighters demoralized and in disarray, many rebels went over to the government side.

In early 1919, word reached Zapata of a disagreement at his enemies' headquarters. General Pablo González had ordered one of his best young cavalry officers, Colonel Jesús Guajardo, to lead a patrol in the hills, but several hours later González had caught him drinking in a local tavern. Guajardo escaped through the back door, but González caught up with him and had him arrested and jailed. Although he was later reinstated in his command, it was rumored that the young officer bitterly resented being jailed by González. Zapata sent Guajardo a letter suggesting that he come over to the Zapatistas with all his troops.

The letter was intercepted by González. This was his chance to get rid of Zapata at last. He called for Guajardo, kept him waiting in an outer room throughout dinner, then had him brought in while coffee was being served. As Guajardo stood at attention, González calmly accused him of being a traitor. Showing him Zapata's letter as proof of his betrayal, González so violently threatened Guajardo with a court martial and a firing squad that the young colonel broke down in tears. Then González offered him a chance to redeem himself. He could accept the invitation, play along with it, and lead Zapata into a trap. Guajardo agreed. Standing in front of González, he wrote out a reply to Zapata in which he agreed to defect. He also offered to bring with him his entire unit and a large quantity of ammunition.

When Zapata received Guajardo's letter, the Zapatista generals advised caution. They did not trust Guajardo; his offer seemed too good to be true. But Zapata, hoping for help in light of his movement's desperate military situation, decided to accept Gua-

House-to-house fighting during the revolution. By 1919, some 45 percent of Morelos's population had been killed, starved to death, deported, or had fled the state. Historians estimate that the Mexican Revolution claimed the lives of more than 1 million people between 1910 and 1919.

jardo's offer. The ammunition Guajardo offered to bring was badly needed, and with it Zapata might be able to retake the entire state again, as he had done in the winter of 1916–17. The national situation was very unstable, and a rift between Obregón and Carranza was already evident. One more Zapatista success might act as a spark, setting off the explosion that would bring down Carranza. No one knows exactly what went through Zapata's mind, but it is known that he took unaccustomed personal risks in his effort to bring about Guajardo's defection.

On April 7, 1919, Guajardo "revolted" as agreed and took the town of Jonacatepec while Zapatista forces made diversionary attacks on several other targets. As proof of his loyalty, Zapata had asked Guajardo to arrest a group of former Zapatistas who had gone over to the government side. Guajardo not only made the arrest — he had them shot as well. He then headed south toward a railway station outside of town where he would meet Zapata.

The two leaders were supposed to come with escorts of only 30 soldiers apiece, but Guajardo brought all 600 men under his command, as well as a mounted machine gun. Zapata met him anyway. Guajardo explained that he could not be sure his men would remain loyal to him if he left them behind in the town. He presented Zapata with a beautiful horse called the Golden Ace but acted strained and refused to join the Zapatistas for a meal, complaining that he had a stomachache. After a conference, Guajardo suggested that it would be best if he returned to town to safeguard the ammunition he had stockpiled there. The two men agreed to meet the next day at Chinameca Hacienda.

Zapata camped in the hills that night, received reinforcements of about 150 men, and arrived at Chinameca Hacienda at 8:30 A.M. the next day. He and Guajardo were holding a conference in one of the buildings outside the hacienda walls, when they were interrupted by reports that enemy troops had been seen nearby. Zapata ordered Guajardo to guard the hacienda while he and his men went to scout the area.

Zapata having disappeared, Zapatismo has died.
—PABLO GONZÁLEZ

Zapata returned at about 1:30 P.M., having found no government troops. He stopped with some of his men at one of the buildings outside the hacienda walls. Some of Guajardo's officers arrived to invite him into the hacienda for lunch. Zapata hesitated, then decided to go into the compound.

A little after 2:00 P.M. Zapata entered the hacienda, riding through the gates on Golden Ace. He was escorted by only 10 of his men. Inside the walls, Guajardo's troops were drawn up in ranks like an honor guard. Zapata rode forward to the front porch of the hacienda building, dismounted, and walked toward the steps.

A bugler sounded the honor call. At the end of the third note the soldiers of the honor guard raised their guns and fired two volleys into Zapata's back. The surprise was complete. Unable to turn around or even to get his pistol out of its holster, Zapata pitched violently forward, his face crashing into the hacienda steps. He was dead.

A 1922 procession marking the third anniversary of Zapata's assassination. In April 1919, Zapata was shot in the back by an honor guard of troops the revolutionary leader had been led to believe was defecting to his side.

8

The Dream Lives On

At first, the people of Morelos refused to believe that Zapata was dead. His body was brought to the main square of Cuautla and dumped on the ground for all to see, but everyone insisted it was not really Zapata. There was a birthmark, a scar, or some other identifying mark that this body did not have. It looked like Zapata, but it was not really him. He had been seen in the mountains, alone, they said, riding one of the spirited horses he always liked. The villagers desperately needed to believe that Zapata was not dead, and the belief persisted that he had somehow gotten away and would return to protect them.

The Zapatista commanders knew very well that Zapata was dead, but they held the movement together with a remarkable unity of purpose. They soon met and elected a new leader, Gildardo Magaña, Zapata's wise young chief of staff who had been so efficient at making political contacts.

Rebels of the South it is better to die on your feet than to live on your knees.
—inscription carved on a post and dated the day after Zapata's murder

A depiction of Zapata by the great Mexican painter and muralist Diego Rivera. After his death, Zapata became a legendary figure who fired the Mexican imagination. By the 1930s, the reforms he had championed were adopted throughout Mexico.

Álvaro Obregón, Mexico's president from 1920 to 1924. In 1920, Obregón, the Zapatistas, and other revolutionaries overthrew Carranza, who was killed as he tried to flee the country. Obregón, whose rise to power marked the end of the fighting, began to institute many of Zapata's reforms.

Within a year, those contacts paid off when the moderate northerner Álvaro Obregón revolted against Carranza. Obregón had been Carranza's best general, but he had always been much more sympathetic to agrarian causes and much more flexible than Carranza.

Carranza could not tolerate this active, capable leader whose popularity grew rapidly during and after the revolution. When Obregón announced that he would run for president in 1920, Carranza had him arrested and put on trial in Mexico City. But Obregón was ready. He was in contact with his supporters, with the unions, with the leaders in the north — and with the Zapatistas, through Gildardo Magaña and Genevevo de la O. With the help of the railway workers' union he made a dramatic escape from Mexico City disguised as a railway brakeman and headed deep into Zapatista territory in Morelos and Guerrero, where he was received with open arms. Genevevo de la O led a raid of 500 Zapatistas into the suburbs of Mexico City to rescue Obregón's second-in-command, General Benjamín Hill, bringing him back to de la O's camp in the mountains of northern Morelos. Within a month, most of northern and southwestern Mexico had risen in revolt against Carranza, who fled Mexico City with the national treasury on a train bound for Veracruz. He was assassinated en route.

Obregón triumphantly returned to Mexico City, accompanied by de la O, Magaña, and the Zapatistas who had helped his revolt to succeed. This time, the Zapatistas had really won. Obregón gave them complete control of the government of Morelos. Dr. José Parrés, who had served as Zapata's medical officer, was named governor of the state. De la O was appointed the state's military commander, and Magaña became an important national politician, actively involved in agrarian reform.

During the next few years Morelos underwent the most extensive land reform program in Mexico. Villages throughout the state brought out old deeds to reclaim their land from the haciendas, and the first village to file suit under the new agricultural decrees was Anenecuilco, which was still fighting for the same lands it had lost when Zapata was a young man. Rural schools were built and pension funds were set up for the widows and orphans of Zapatistas killed during the revolution. Large tracts of land were taken from the haciendas and redistributed to the villages and small farmers; the hacienda owners were compensated with government bonds. By 1927, according to American historian John Womack, "80 percent of the state's farming families now held fields of their own, which altogether amounted to around 75 percent of the arable land." Morelos was still poor and backward, but it was at peace, and the majority of its people had gained greater personal control over their lives. When a revolt broke out against the government in 1923, Genevevo de la O held the state solidly behind Obregón. The revolutions were over for Morelos.

Land reform faltered and corruption set in during the late 1920s, but in 1934 Lázaro Cárdenas, the young boy who had run off to join Madero when he was only 15 years old, became president of Mexico. More than anyone else, he helped to realize Zapata's dreams of land reform, extending the programs that had been instituted in Morelos to other parts of the country. During his term, rural schools were built, farm cooperatives were organized, extensive rural public-works programs were begun, and Mexico instituted one of the most extensive land reform programs in the world. The fruits of this reform are still debated by agricultural experts, but it is certain that life for millions of Mexican farmers became significantly better.

Pancho Villa stands next to U.S. general John Pershing in 1920. The former antagonists met when the Mexican government awarded Villa a large ranch and persuaded him to retire from politics and warfare. Villa was assassinated in July 1923.

During the next two decades the Cárdenas reforms helped to make the Mexican rural economy one of the most productive and dynamic in the developing world. Large-scale commercial agriculture returned to many areas, particularly in northern Mexico, but the abuses of the past were not repeated. Mexicans throughout the country shared a rising standard of living and rising expectations.

But Cárdenas's successors were not as idealistic as he had been, and the ruling party in Mexico once more became mired in corruption as the old patterns of repression returned. By the 1960s Mexico faced enormous economic and social problems, due in large part to one of the most rapid population increases in world history. Mexico's population to-

Lázaro Cárdenas, who had joined the revolution in 1911 as a 15 year old, descends from a train after becoming president in 1934. Cárdenas was renowned for his progressive agrarian and labor laws as well as his recognition of Indian rights. His son Cuauhtémoc ran for president as a reform candidate in 1988.

day is more than five times greater than it was in 1910; Mexico City, the most populous in the world, is surrounded by massive shantytowns, the result of uncontrolled growth and the mass migration of the rural population to the city. The Mexican economy has been destroyed by the falling price of petroleum, runaway inflation, rampant corruption, and the catastrophic drop in the international exchange value of the peso. True, the standard of living has declined in most Latin American countries since the 1960s, but the decline has been particularly severe in Mexico, where extensive rural and urban poverty once again pose enormous problems. In the 1988 elections the ruling party in Mexico was seriously challenged for the first time in many years. Interestingly enough, one of the main challengers was Cuauhtémoc Cárdenas, the son of Lázaro Cárdenas, the man who carried out many of the land reforms first proposed by the Zapatistas.

From a historical point of view in the world at large, the Zapatista revolution was very important because it was one of the first of the great peasant revolutions of the 20th century. Previous revolutions, particularly in 19th century Europe, had been based in the cities. But in the 20th century a wave of agrarian-based revolutions swept the underdeveloped world, from Mexico to Russia, from China to Africa and Southeast Asia.

Like the Zapatista revolution, many of the 20th-century peasant revolutions were born of the discontent caused by the rapid destruction of traditional rural societies. The late 19th and early 20th centuries saw the spread of European colonies and the development of railroads, steamship lines, and large-scale commercial agriculture throughout the world. As in Morelos, the introduction of this new form of agriculture was often a very brutal, rapid process that destroyed the traditional rural society of small peasant farmers. The resulting disruption and dislocation, and the resentment of foreign intervention it fostered, paved the way for the peasant revolutions of the 20th century.

The Zapatista revolution was thus a portent of the events that would occur throughout the underdeveloped world in the years that followed. In Mexico, Zapata himself became a powerful symbol, a legend. His story was told again and again in Mexican popular songs, and he became an almost mythical figure in modern Mexican art, in paintings such as those of the great muralist Diego Rivera.

The land belongs to those who work it.
—EMILIANO ZAPATA

Mexico has changed so dramatically since 1910 that the specific solutions proposed by the Zapatistas during the Mexican Revolution may no longer be appropriate today. But there is no question that during the 40 years following Zapata's death, the land reforms he and his followers fought for significantly improved the lives of millions of people in rural Mexico. If the struggle goes on today to provide a decent life for the Mexican people, it is still Zapata's leadership and stubborn integrity that have provided the example. It is still Zapata's angry voice that echoes down to us through the years, demanding "Land and Liberty" for the desperately impoverished peoples of the underdeveloped world.

Further Reading

Alba, Victor. *The Mexicans.* New York: Pegasus, 1967.

Brenner, Anita, and George R. Leighton. *The Wind that Swept Mexico.* New York: Harper & Row, 1943.

Katz, Friedrich. *The Secret War in Mexico: Europe, the United States and the Mexican Revolution.* Chicago: University of Chicago Press, 1981.

King, Rosa. *Tempest over Mexico: A Personal Chronicle.* Boston: Little, Brown, 1940.

Lewis, Oscar. *Life in a Mexican Village: Tepoztlan Restudied.* Urbana: University of Illinois Press, 1951.

———. *Pedro Martinez: A Mexican Peasant and his Family.* New York: Random House, 1964.

Mason, Herbert Molloy, Jr. *The Great Pursuit.* New York: Random House, 1970.

Newell, G. Roberto, and F. Luis Rubio. *Mexico's Dilemma: The Political Origins of Economic Crisis.* Boulder, CO: Westview Press, 1984.

Parkes, Henry Bamford. *A History of Mexico.* Boston: Houghton Mifflin, 1960.

Parkinson, Roger. *Zapata.* New York: Stein & Day, 1975.

Perry, Laurens Ballard. *Juárez and Díaz: Machine Politics in Mexico.* Dekalb: Northern Illinois Press, 1978.

Reed, John. *Insurgent Mexico.* New York: International Publishers, 1970.

Tannenbaum, Frank. *Peace by Revolution: An Interpretation of Mexico.* New York: Knopf, 1956.

Turner, John Kenneth. *Barbarous Mexico.* Austin: University of Texas Press, 1969.

Wepman, Dennis. *Benito Juárez.* New York: Chelsea House, 1986.

Womack, John, Jr. *Zapata and the Mexican Revolution.* New York: Vintage, 1969.

Chronology

ca. 1879	Born Emiliano Zapata in state of Morelos, Mexico
1909	Elected president of the village council of Anenecuilco
1910	Francisco Madero runs for president; President Porfirio Díaz imprisons Madero, who then escapes; revolt breaks out in northern Mexico; Zapata begins to occupy land in the state of Morelos
March 11, 1911	Zapata begins revolt in Villa de Ayala
May 1911	Treaty of Ciudad Juárez; Madero overthrows the Díaz government; Díaz leaves Mexico
June 7, 1911	Madero enters Mexico City; meets Zapata
Aug. 1911	Federal army enters Morelos; Zapata flees to the mountains of Puebla
Oct. 1911	Madero elected president of Mexico
Nov. 1911	Inauguration of Madero; he and Zapata fail to reach a land-reform agreement
Nov. 28, 1911	Zapata issues the Plan of Ayala
1912	Military struggle continues in Morelos
Feb. 1913	A coup d'état ousts Madero; General Victoriano Huerta assumes the presidency
April 21, 1914	The United States invades and then occupies Veracruz
July 1914	Huerta resigns and leaves Mexico
Aug. 1914	Carranza occupies Mexico City
Oct. 1914	Convention of revolutionary leaders rejects Carranza and calls for new elections
Nov. 1914	Carranza's forces flee to Veracruz; Pancho Villa and his troops press further south
Nov. 24, 1914	Zapata occupies Mexico City
Dec. 4, 1914	Meets Villa in Xochimilco
1915	Zapatistas carry out agrarian reform in Morelos
Dec. 1915–May 1916	Carranza's forces retake Morelos
Dec. 1916–Feb. 1917	Zapata's forces retake Morelos
Nov. 1917–Jan. 1919	Carranza's forces retake most of Morelos
April 10, 1919	Zapata killed in an ambush

Index

John David Ragan received his M.A. in French from the University of Cincinnati and is currently working toward a Ph.D. in history at New York University, where one of his specialties is agrarian issues. He has worked, traveled, or studied in more than 30 countries, seeking out numerous adventures, including winter oil-exploration off the Alaskan coast, bicycle and motorcycle tours of Europe, and hiking in the Himalayas.

Arthur M. Schlesinger, jr., taught history at Harvard for many years and is currently Albert Schweitzer Professor of the Humanities at City University of New York. He is the author of numerous highly praised works in American history and has twice been awarded the Pulitzer Prize. He served in the White House as special assistant to Presidents Kennedy and Johnson.

PICTURE CREDITS

The Bettmann Archive: pp. 2, 12, 22, 30, 45, 60, 62, 64, 69, 76, 77, 78, 86, 87, 93, 96, 104, 105, 106; Brown Brothers: pp. 14, 28, 32, 40, 42, 53, 56, 70; Centro De Estudios Sobre La Universidad, UNAM: pp. 21, 38, 46, 82, 94, 99; Culver Pictures: pp. 15, 16, 20, 24, 25, 34, 36, 51, 54, 57, 65, 67, 68, 72, 74, 80, 81, 88, 90, 95, 97, 100, 102; Library of Congress: pp. 18, 19, 58, 84; Donna Sinisgalli: p. 27; The Wheelan Collection, University Archives, Texas A&M University, College Station, Texas: pp. 48, 63, 66, 83